Tax Lien Money Making Machine

Maximizing Property Taxes Investment Returns

KAITLIN HENDERSON

Copyright

Why Should You Read This Book

I am Kaitlin Henderson, I am an internationally acclaimed and bestselling personal finance author, lecturer, and advisor. Through my work, I have dedicated myself to teaching people to manage their money better and to successfully direct their own investments.

I am a former management consultant to businesses for which I helped improve operations and profitability. Before, during, and after my time of working crazy hours and traveling too much, I had the good sense to focus on financial matters.

I have spent more than three decades working in various capacities in the financial markets. I first invested in mutual funds back in the mid-1980s, when i opened a mutual fund account at Fidelity With the assistance of Dr. Martin Zweig, a well-known analyst of the financial markets.

In addition to investing in securities over the decades, i have also successfully invested in real estate and started and managed my own business. I have offered advice to thousands of clients on a range of investment conundrums and concerns.

I earned a bachelor's degree in economics at Yale and an MBA at the Stanford Graduate School of Business. Despite these impediments to lucid reasoning, I came to my senses and decided that life was too short to spend it working long hours and waiting in airports for the benefit of larger companies.

Table of Contents

Introduction to Tax Lien Investing

In the vast realm of investment opportunities, few can match the sheer potential and power of Tax Lien. Welcome to the world of "Tax Lien Money Making Machine: Maximizing Property Taxes Investment Returns," where we embark on a journey that promises both financial prosperity and investment enlightenment.

Unlocking the Power of Tax Lien

In a world where financial security is paramount, Tax Lien emerge as an unsung hero. In this inaugural chapter, we delve into the heart of Tax Lien, revealing a financial instrument that has the potential to revolutionize the way you perceive investments.

Understanding Tax Lien

At its core, a tax lien represents an investment in a property owner's unpaid tax debt. When property owners fall behind on their tax payments, local governments issue Tax Lien to secure the owed funds. These liens, in turn, become available to savvy investors like you. But why should you consider Tax Lien as a means to maximize your investment returns?

The Power of Tax Lien

Tax Lien are not just financial instruments; they are the gateway to unlocking significant returns and creating lasting wealth. Their appeal lies in their unique characteristics, making them a "money-making machine" of sorts.

Security: Tax Lien are secured by the property itself. This means that your investment is backed by a tangible asset, reducing your risk significantly.

Attractive Returns: Tax Lien offer interest rates that can soar well into the double digits. In an era of low-yield investments, the potential for high returns sets Tax Lien apart.

First Position: In the event of non-payment, Tax Lien take precedence over other liens or claims, putting you in a strong position to recover your investment.

Recession-Proof: Tax Lien have proven their resilience through economic downturns, offering stability when traditional investments can falter.

Local Impact: By investing in Tax Lien, you are directly contributing to local communities' well-being, aiding in the funding of essential public services.

Empowerment: Tax lien investing empowers you to take control of your financial future, create wealth, and secure your legacy.

What to Expect from This Book

As you embark on this journey of tax lien investment exploration, "Tax Lien Money Making Machine" promises to equip you with the knowledge and strategies to transform your financial landscape. It's not just about investing; it's about optimizing property taxes to enhance your investment returns.

In the chapters to come, we will dive deeper into the tax lien landscape, understanding the intricacies, and revealing advanced techniques to maximize your returns. We will explore the processes of acquiring Tax Lien, realizing returns, and navigating the complexities that may arise. Most importantly, you will discover how to utilize Tax Lien as a "money-making machine" that can fuel your financial dreams.

But it doesn't stop at financial prosperity. Tax lien investing offers an opportunity to contribute positively to your local community. By investing in Tax Lien, you are not only growing your wealth but also supporting the infrastructure and services that benefit everyone.

"Tax Lien Money Making Machine" aims to be your ultimate guide to realizing the untapped potential of Tax Lien. This book will not only provide you with valuable insights and knowledge but will also serve as a catalyst for transforming your approach to investment.

As you read further, you will explore the ins and outs of tax lien investments, learning about the different types of liens, strategies for acquiring them, and ways to handle non-payment situations. By the end of your journey, you will be equipped with the tools and confidence to make Tax Lien a vital component of your investment portfolio.

It's time to embark on a journey that can truly transform your financial future. This book is your key to maximizing property tax investment returns, empowering you to become a savvy and prosperous investor. So, get ready to unlock the hidden potential of Tax Lien and turn your investment dreams into a reality.

Chapter 1: The Tax Lien Investment Landscape

Tax Lien Opportunities, Discovery, and Treasures

Imagine a market where returns can soar into the double digits, where security is backed by tangible assets, and where recession-proof investment opportunities abound. That's the tax lien market for you. As we delve into this chapter, we'll uncover the unique characteristics that make tax lien investments a hidden gem in the investment world.

One of the most intriguing aspects of Tax Lien is that they are typically issued by local governments. This makes tax lien investments a compelling way to contribute positively to your local community while securing your financial future. When property owners fall behind on their taxes, local governments issue Tax Lien to recoup the funds they're owed.

Furthermore, at the heart of every tax lien is a piece of real estate, a tangible asset with intrinsic value. This property serves as collateral for your investment. In the event of non-payment by the property owner, you could claim ownership of the property itself, opening up the door to significant financial gains.

Types of Tax Lien

As we continue our journey through this landscape, you'll discover that there are different types of Tax Lien. The most common ones include:

Property Tax Lien

These are the most prevalent and offer a stable investment opportunity. When property owners fail to pay their property taxes, a lien is issued on the property, making it an attractive target for investors.

Municipal Tax Lien

These liens are linked to unpaid municipal charges such as water bills or fees. The investor has the potential to receive the amount paid for the lien, plus interest.

Special Assessment Tax Lien

These are associated with specific community projects like road construction or sewer improvements. Investing in these liens can lead to attractive returns.

Investment-Grade Tax Lien

These are highly sought after for their security and guaranteed returns. They are considered a safe haven for investors looking for reliable income.

Strategies for Success

In this captivating landscape, strategies are your compass. To maximize property tax investment returns, it's crucial to have a well-thought-out approach. In "Tax Lien Money Making Machine," we reveal proven strategies that can help you navigate and thrive in this terrain.

Acquisition Strategies

You'll learn how to identify Tax Lien that align with your investment goals. We'll explore ways to research and select liens that offer maximum potential for returns.

Management Techniques

Effective management of your tax lien portfolio is essential. Our book provides insights into tracking and managing your investments to ensure they grow and prosper.

Non-Payment Resolution

While the tax lien landscape is filled with opportunities, it's not without its challenges. "Tax Lien Money Making Machine" equips you with the knowledge to address non-payment situations and take appropriate actions.

It's time to take that step forward into a world where returns are impressive, opportunities are abundant, and financial security is achievable. In the next chapter, we will explore the acquisition of Tax Lien, revealing strategies to make the most out of this incredible landscape. Get ready for a life-changing journey that can truly transform your financial future!

Examining the Current Tax Lien

Investment Market

In this engaging segment, we delve into the heart of the matter - the current tax lien investment market. Here, we'll explore why the market is more enticing than ever, uncover its growth prospects, and why now is the ideal time to seize this investment opportunity.

The Tax Lien Investment Market: A Thriving Ecosystem

The tax lien investment market has been evolving and thriving, offering investors opportunities like never before. This dynamic ecosystem is influenced by various factors, all of which work together to make it a lucrative investment landscape.

1. Economic Volatility and Tax Lien

One of the key factors contributing to the attractiveness of tax lien investments is the economic volatility. In uncertain economic times, investors seek stable and secure options, which Tax Lien inherently provide. The market's stable returns are often unaffected by stock market fluctuations or economic downturns.

2. Growing Investor Interest

The tax lien market is experiencing a surge in investor interest, making it more competitive than ever. Investors, both experienced and newcomers, are increasingly recognizing the potential for substantial returns. This heightened competition is driving innovation and opportunities for investors.

3. Lower Barrier to Entry

As governments seek to recoup overdue property taxes efficiently, they've made it easier for investors to participate in tax lien auctions. This lower barrier to entry is opening doors for a wider range of investors, making it a more inclusive and diverse market.

4. Real Estate Value

The market's foundation lies in real estate. As real estate values continue to appreciate over time, the collateral underlying Tax Lien becomes more valuable. This growth is good news for investors, as the chances of acquiring a valuable property through tax lien foreclosure increase.

Profitable Opportunities Await

As we explore the current tax lien market in this chapter, you'll soon realize that profitable opportunities await. In "Tax Lien Money Making Machine," we delve into various aspects that make these investments particularly attractive:

Diversification: Tax Lien offer a unique way to diversify your investment portfolio. Unlike traditional investments, they are backed by tangible assets, reducing your risk.

Predictable Returns: The market provides predictable, stable returns, often in the form of fixed interest rates. This predictability is a sought-after quality in the investment world.

Security Backed by Real Estate: Every tax lien is tied to real estate, offering security in the form of tangible property. If the property owner defaults, you have the opportunity to acquire the property at a fraction of its market value.

Local Community Involvement: By investing in Tax Lien, you're actively participating in your local community's financial well-being. Your investment helps support essential public services, making you a valued contributor.

Embracing Tax Lien: A Wise Decision

In a world of financial uncertainty, making a wise decision about where to invest your hard-earned money is crucial. The tax lien investment market's stability, predictability, and opportunities make it an attractive option.

The Right Time for Tax Lien Investments

Timing is essential in investing, and now is an ideal time to consider Tax Lien. As we delve deeper into the chapters of this book, you'll gain insights into the acquisition process, management techniques, and strategies for maximizing your returns.

Investors who understand the potential of the current tax lien market are well-poised to reap the rewards. The opportunities in this investment landscape are like hidden treasures, waiting to be discovered by those who dare to explore.

Historical Performance and Trends

In this segment, we'll embark on a journey through time, exploring the historical performance and trends of tax lien investments. By understanding the past, we can gain valuable insights into the promising future of this investment opportunity.

The Lessons of History

History has always been an excellent teacher. When it comes to investments, understanding the historical performance of an asset class is invaluable. Tax lien investments are no exception, and they have a rich historical backdrop that offers profound insights into their potential.

Early Tax Lien Systems

The concept of Tax Lien and their usage dates back centuries. Historically, they have been an essential tool for governments to collect overdue property taxes efficiently. The tax lien system allows local municipalities to recover lost revenue by selling Tax Lien to investors.

Tax Lien have consistently demonstrated their worth as an investment class. Throughout history, their performance has been stable, with consistent returns for those who understand the dynamics of the market. This chapter delves into the historical returns and trends that make tax lien investments so appealing today.

Consistent Returns Over Time

One of the most remarkable aspects of tax lien investments is their consistent performance over time. Historical data reveals that Tax Lien have provided reliable returns even during economic recessions and market volatility.

Investors who participated in tax lien auctions in the past often secured Tax Lien with attractive interest rates. These interest rates are fixed and guaranteed by local governments. Such consistent and secured returns are a rarity in the investment world, making Tax Lien an attractive option for those seeking financial stability.

Protection Against Economic Uncertainty

Historical performance also highlights the resilience of tax lien investments in times of economic uncertainty. When stock markets were plummeting, and financial crises were looming, investors who had diversified into Tax Lien enjoyed stable returns.

Tax lien investments provide a unique form of protection. They are backed by tangible assets - the underlying real estate properties. If the property owner fails to pay the overdue taxes, investors have the opportunity to acquire the property at a fraction of its market value. This asset-backed security is one of the key reasons behind the historical success of Tax Lien.

Growing Popularity in Modern Times

The historical trends in tax lien investments indicate their growing popularity. In recent years, there has been a significant increase in the number of investors exploring this asset class. This surge in interest is fueled by the track record of stable returns and the security offered by Tax Lien.

Additionally, governments at all levels are recognizing the benefits of using Tax Lien to efficiently collect overdue property taxes. This recognition has made it easier for investors to access tax lien auctions and participate in this thriving market.

Positioning for the Future

As we delve deeper into the chapters of "Tax Lien Money Making Machine," you'll learn how to position yourself for the future by leveraging the lessons of history. You'll discover strategies to maximize your returns, minimize risks, and secure your financial future.

In the investment world, those who understand the historical performance of asset classes are better equipped to make informed decisions. Tax lien investments, with their rich history of consistent returns and asset-backed security, are a compelling option for both seasoned and novice investors.

The historical performance and trends of Tax Lien present a compelling case for their inclusion in your investment portfolio. The lessons of the past reveal that Tax Lien are not just an investment option but a financial instrument that offers stability, security, and growth potential.

As you continue your journey through this book, you'll gain deeper insights into the strategies and techniques that will enable you to make the most of this extraordinary investment opportunity. Get ready to shape your financial future by learning from the past and seizing the potential of tax lien investments. The future awaits, and it's full of promise for those who dare to explore it!

Recognizing Opportunities and Challenges

Let's explore the opportunities and challenges that await astute investors. By recognizing these factors, you'll be better equipped to navigate the intriguing terrain of tax lien investing.

Seizing Opportunities

Investors are drawn to tax lien investments for a variety of compelling reasons. Among the most enticing opportunities are:

1. Attractive Returns: Tax Lien offer investors the prospect of high fixed interest rates, often far surpassing those of traditional investments like savings accounts or CDs. These attractive yields make Tax Lien an appealing option for those seeking significant returns on their investments.

2. Asset-Backed Security: Tax lien investments are backed by real estate properties. In the event of default by the property owner, investors have the potential to acquire the property at a substantial discount. This asset-backed security sets Tax Lien apart from many other investment options.

3. Diversification: Tax lien investments provide diversification within your investment portfolio. Diversifying across asset classes can help minimize risk, and Tax Lien offer a unique alternative to traditional stocks and bonds.

4. Low Competition: Surprisingly, the tax lien market often sees less competition compared to other investment classes. This provides investors with a significant advantage, as fewer competitors can lead to higher chances of securing lucrative Tax Lien.

5. Government Support: Governments at various levels have recognized the advantages of tax lien investments. They have streamlined the process, making it more accessible for investors. The support of local municipalities and governments enhances the credibility and security of tax lien investments.

Overcoming Challenges

While tax lien investments offer a plethora of opportunities, it's vital to acknowledge the potential challenges:

1. Due Diligence: Research is key to successful tax lien investments. Investors need to thoroughly examine the properties associated with Tax Lien, assess their value, and be aware of any potential issues. Failing to conduct due diligence can lead to unforeseen challenges.

2. Legal Complexity: Tax lien investments involve legal intricacies. Investors need to understand local laws, redemption periods, and the legal processes governing Tax Lien in their chosen jurisdictions. Legal knowledge is essential for successful tax lien investing.

3. Property Conditions: The physical state of properties associated with Tax Lien can vary significantly. Investors may encounter properties in various conditions, from well-maintained to those in need of extensive renovation. Assessing property conditions and estimating repair costs is crucial.

4. Default Risk: While Tax Lien are relatively secure investments, there is a default risk associated with property owners failing to pay their overdue taxes. Investors need to be prepared for the possibility of acquiring properties through this process.

5. Competing Bids: Though less competitive than some other investments, tax lien auctions can still attract multiple bids for desirable properties. Understanding the auction dynamics and employing effective bidding strategies is essential.

The Path Forward

As you continue your journey through this book, you'll gain invaluable insights into identifying the most promising opportunities while effectively addressing the challenges. Tax lien investments offer a unique combination of high returns, asset-backed security, and diversification potential.

This segment underscores the importance of recognizing the landscape of tax lien investments. By acknowledging the opportunities and challenges, you are better prepared to harness the full potential of this investment class. As you explore the pages ahead, you'll discover strategies and techniques to seize opportunities while mitigating challenges.

With optimism and a well-informed approach, you can make tax lien investments a cornerstone of your financial success. Stay committed to your investment education and remember that the path to financial prosperity is built on knowledge and informed decisions.

As you venture further into this book, you'll unlock the secrets of tax lien investing, equipping yourself with the tools to navigate the opportunities and challenges in this dynamic market. Welcome to a world of financial possibilities and the exciting journey of maximizing property tax investment returns. Your future as a savvy tax lien investor is bright, and every chapter brings you closer to realizing your financial aspirations.

Chapter 2: Getting Started in Tax Lien Investing

As you embark on this chapter, you'll discover that the realm of tax lien investing offers endless opportunities for investors seeking attractive returns, asset-backed security, and diversification. The world of Tax Lien is not reserved for seasoned investors alone. It's a welcoming space for newcomers who are ready to make their money work for them.

The Prerequisites for Becoming a Tax Lien Investor

As you venture into the exhilarating world of tax lien investments, it's crucial to understand that these prerequisites are your steppingstones to a lucrative financial future. Each requirement is a building block, a foundation for your success in the realm of Tax Lien.

Knowledge is Key

The journey to becoming a proficient tax lien investor begins with knowledge. This is your most valuable prerequisite. In the investment world, the adage "knowledge is power" holds true. You must educate yourself about the intricacies of tax lien investing, legal regulations, and property markets.

1. Education: Start by immersing yourself in books, courses, and online resources dedicated to Tax Lien. These learning materials will equip you with the vital knowledge you need to make informed decisions. The deeper your understanding, the more confidently you can navigate the tax lien landscape.

2. Legal Expertise: Tax lien investments involve navigating complex legal waters. Understanding the legal framework, including redemption periods and property laws, is essential. Legal expertise ensures that you are well-prepared to make sound investment decisions within the confines of the law.

Research and Due Diligence

The second set of prerequisites revolves around research and due diligence. Once you've armed yourself with knowledge, it's time to put it into practice.

3. Due Diligence: Researching potential tax lien properties and the local market is paramount. This involves assessing property values, understanding market demand, and identifying potential challenges. Conducting due diligence is your guard against making uninformed investment choices.

4. Bidding Strategies: Developing effective bidding strategies is the next step. You must discern when to bid aggressively and when to exercise restraint. This skill comes with experience, but with your solid foundation of knowledge, you can start crafting your winning strategies right away.

Financial Prerequisites

Financial readiness is another cornerstone of becoming a successful tax lien investor. To make your mark in the tax lien arena, you must be financially prepared.

5. Investment Capital: Tax Lien require capital, as you'll be purchasing property liens from delinquent property owners. Assess your financial situation and set aside an investment budget. The level of capital can vary, and there are options for investors with various budgets.

6. Reserve Funds: It's prudent to maintain a reserve fund for unforeseen expenses. Tax lien investments may sometimes require additional funds for property maintenance, legal matters, or unexpected costs.

Patience and Persistence

7. Patience: Rome wasn't built in a day, and neither is a lucrative tax lien portfolio. It's important to have realistic expectations. Tax lien investments may not yield immediate returns, but with patience, your investments can grow and thrive over time.

8. Persistence: The path to financial prosperity isn't always a straight line. Setbacks and challenges can be part of the journey. Persistence and the ability to persevere through difficulties are prerequisites for success. With a persistent attitude, you can overcome obstacles and maximize your investment returns.

Your Path to Prosperity

The optimism that flows through the pages of this chapter is your guide. It's your reminder that with each prerequisite you fulfill, you move one step closer to realizing your financial dreams. Tax lien investing is an open door, and you possess the keys to unlock it. Your readiness, persistence, and knowledge have brought you to this chapter, and the future beckons.

So, as you delve into the world of tax lien investments, remember that you're not alone on this journey. The prerequisites are your allies, and they stand ready to support your aspirations for financial growth. As you absorb the knowledge, embrace the research, and prepare financially, you're setting the stage for a rewarding adventure into tax lien investing.

Understanding the Legal and Regulatory Framework

It is time we dive into the crucial foundation of tax lien investing —understanding the legal and regulatory framework. Knowledge is power, and here, we empower you with insights into the laws and regulations that govern this lucrative investment avenue.

The Legal Landscape

Tax lien investing, like any financial endeavor, operates within a framework of legal statutes and regulations. These laws vary from state to state and even between local jurisdictions. In this chapter, we explore the legal landscape with optimism and a clear perspective.

Understanding Legal Jurisdictions

State Regulations: Each state has its own set of rules and regulations governing tax lien sales. It is vital to comprehend these state-specific laws before entering the world of tax lien investing.

County and Municipal Laws: Furthermore, even within a state, counties and municipalities may have unique laws related to tax lien sales. Chapter 6 provides an insightful guide to navigating these intricacies.

The Due Diligence Imperative

A critical theme in this chapter is the due diligence imperative. We advocate a proactive and diligent approach to research. Optimism in the investment world is often a result of thorough preparation. With detailed information on tax lien auctions and related processes, you gain the upper hand.

Due Diligence Components

Property Assessment: We delve into the importance of property assessment, understanding how to appraise potential tax lien investments, and the role of the assessor's office in this process.

Redemption Periods: Each jurisdiction has its redemption periods, which vary from a few months to several years. These periods impact your investment strategy, and we explore them in detail.

Interest Rates: Interest rates on Tax Lien are a key determinant of your returns. This segment offers optimism through an exploration of how these rates are calculated and their impact on your investments.

Legal Safeguards

Optimism in the world of tax lien investing is also founded on legal safeguards. These safeguards are designed to protect your investments and ensure a fair and just process.

Right to Redemption: We outline the concept of the right to redemption, which provides property owners with an opportunity to pay their taxes and redeem their property from tax lien investors.

Penalties for Non-Redemption: The legal framework often includes penalties for property owners who do not redeem their properties within the specified period.

Foreclosure Procedures: In the event of non-redemption, the legal system outlines the process of foreclosure and property transfer.

We clarify the steps involved, ensuring you are well informed.

Through an optimistic lens, we see that the legal landscape, due diligence, safeguards, and compliance considerations are the pillars upon which you build your journey to financial prosperity. With this chapter as your guide, you are better equipped to navigate the complexities of tax lien investing, secure your investments, and maximize your returns.

The legal and regulatory framework need not be a hindrance; rather, it is your ally in the realm of tax lien investments. As you delve into this chapter, remember that optimism in investing is often a product of knowledge and preparation. By understanding the laws and regulations that govern tax lien investing, you are poised to transform this venture into a money-making machine.

Chapter 3: Finding the Right Tax Lien

The Quest for Profitable Tax Lien

Optimism is often born from a well-thought-out strategy. In this chapter, we'll guide you through the process of finding the Tax Lien that have the potential to yield profitable returns. The process is akin to searching for hidden treasures, and with the right insights, you can unearth gems.

Tax Lien Listings

Online Resources: We explore the online resources where you can find comprehensive listings of Tax Lien. These include government websites, county records, and specialized tax lien listing services. An optimistic investor knows that the internet is a goldmine of information.

Local Auctions: Another avenue for finding Tax Lien is through local auctions. These auctions provide an opportunity to bid on Tax Lien in person. We emphasize the importance of attending these auctions to see the properties firsthand.

The Art of Due Diligence

Optimism in tax lien investing is closely tied to the due diligence you conduct. We encourage a meticulous approach to evaluating potential investments.

Property Research

Location Matters: The location of a property is a vital factor in determining its value and investment potential. We discuss how to research the local real estate market and assess the desirability of the location.

Property Condition: The condition of a property can significantly impact your investment. By conducting property inspections, you can assess whether it is worth the investment.

Investment Approaches

Diversification: An optimistic investor knows the value of diversification. We explain how spreading your investments across various Tax Lien can reduce risk and enhance profitability.

Niche Opportunities

Optimism often comes from recognizing niche opportunities within an investment avenue. Below are the niche areas where tax lien investing can be particularly rewarding.

Senior Liens: Investing in senior Tax Lien can be a niche opportunity that yields excellent returns.

Commercial Properties: Commercial properties present unique opportunities.

The quest for profitable Tax Lien is akin to a treasure hunt. With the guidance provided in this chapter, you have the map and tools to unearth these treasures. Remember that optimism in tax lien investing is the result of calculated decisions and informed choices.

As you delve further, envision yourself as an explorer in the realm of Tax Lien, navigating uncharted territories and discovering hidden gems. With a well-planned strategy, due diligence, and niche knowledge, you are well on your way to finding the right Tax Lien that will maximize your property taxes investment returns.

Optimism is not blind hope; it is the result of knowledge and strategy. With these tools at your disposal, you are poised to make the right choices in your tax lien investment journey.

Strategies for Sourcing Tax Lien

Optimism is the cornerstone of successful tax lien investing. It's the belief that within this market, there are abundant opportunities waiting to be discovered. The key to unlocking these opportunities lies in your ability to source the right Tax Lien.

Exploring Sourcing Strategies

Local Government Auctions

The world of auctions is a dynamic arena where opportunities and treasures change hands every day. Among these, local government auctions are an intriguing and often overlooked domain. These auctions provide a unique platform where cities and municipalities sell a wide array of items, from surplus equipment to tax-defaulted properties, offering a fascinating glimpse into the heartbeat of the community. In this article, we will delve into the captivating world of local government auctions and discover the hidden gems they offer.

Auctioning the Community's Surplus

Local governments constantly evolve, upgrade, and adapt to meet the changing needs of their residents. This dynamism leads to the accumulation of surplus assets and equipment that are no longer in use but are still in good condition. Instead of accumulating dust in storage, these items find new life at local government auctions.

Municipalities auction a variety of surplus goods, ranging from vehicles and office equipment to furniture and electronics. These auctions are often an excellent opportunity for savvy buyers looking for quality items at a fraction of their market value. From retired police cars to gently used office furniture, the variety of items can be astonishing.

Tax-Defaulted Properties: Real Estate Treasures

One of the most captivating aspects of local government auctions is the sale of tax-defaulted properties. When property owners fail to pay their property taxes, the government places a tax lien on the property. If the taxes remain unpaid, the property may go up for auction to recoup the outstanding debt. This presents a golden opportunity for investors and prospective homeowners.

Local government auctions of tax-defaulted properties can lead to exceptional real estate deals. Properties are often sold at a considerable discount compared to their market value. This means that diligent buyers can acquire homes, land, and commercial properties at a fraction of their actual worth.

Moreover, these auctions often include a diverse range of properties, from suburban homes to urban apartment buildings, providing a broad spectrum of opportunities. While tax lien investing might involve complexities, it can be an exciting way to dive into the real estate market.

Behind the Scenes: The Auction Process

Part of the fascination surrounding local government auctions lies in the intricate process that unfolds. It's an engaging blend of financial strategies, bidding dynamics, and the thrill of discovery.

Here's a simplified glimpse of how a tax lien property auction might work:

Listing: The local government creates a list of tax-defaulted properties scheduled for auction. This list is made public, and interested parties can view the properties available.

Registration: Buyers must register for the auction, often accompanied by a deposit. This ensures that all participants are committed and financially prepared.

Bidding: The auction commences with the bidding process. Bidders compete to secure their desired properties. As the prices rise, the adrenaline surges.

Winning: The highest bidder secures the property. They are then responsible for paying the bid amount and any additional fees.

Ownership Transfer: After the payment is made, the government transfers ownership to the winning bidder, who can then proceed with the property as they see fit.

The thrill of competition, the prospect of discovering a hidden gem, and the satisfaction of landing a fantastic deal all contribute to the allure of local government auctions.

Tips for Success in Local Government Auctions

To navigate this captivating world successfully, consider these tips:

Research Thoroughly: Investigate the properties or items you're interested in. Knowledge is your greatest asset.

Set a Budget: Determine how much you're willing to spend, and stick to your budget. Don't get carried away by the excitement of bidding.

Visit an Auction: If you're new to auctions, attending one in person can provide valuable experience and insights.

Understand the Rules: Make sure you comprehend the specific rules and regulations of the auction you're attending. Each one may have its unique procedures.

Consider Professional Guidance: For tax lien auctions or real estate purchases, consulting with professionals can be a wise move.

Local government auctions are more than just transactions; they are glimpses into the evolving dynamics of a community. They offer unique opportunities for buyers, investors, and curious souls alike. Whether you're on the hunt for a new property or a hidden gem among surplus items, these auctions are captivating windows into the heart of your locality.

So, as you peruse local government auction listings, keep your eyes open for treasures that might be just around the corner, waiting to be uncovered. In the realm of local government auctions, opportunity knocks, and it's an invitation worth accepting.

Tax Lien Brokers

Tax lien brokers serve as knowledgeable intermediaries who navigate the complex world of tax liens and help investors make informed decisions. Let's explore the pivotal role they play in tax lien investments.

The Role of Tax Lien Brokers

Expertise and Local Knowledge

Tax lien brokers are well-versed in the local tax laws and regulations, making them valuable sources of information. They know the ins and outs of the tax lien process in their area, including how to participate in tax lien auctions, what to look for in properties, and the specific rules governing each sale. This local expertise is indispensable for investors, especially those looking to invest in different regions.

Property Evaluation

Brokers assist in evaluating properties associated with tax liens. They can help you identify properties with potential and advise you on the risks and potential rewards. By tapping into their experience and expertise, investors can make well-informed decisions about which tax liens to pursue.

Auction Assistance

Tax lien auctions can be competitive, and understanding the intricacies of bidding and winning bids is essential. Brokers can provide strategies and insights to improve your chances of securing tax liens on promising properties.

Due Diligence

One of the most critical aspects of tax lien investing is conducting thorough due diligence. Tax lien brokers can help you scrutinize the legal and financial aspects of a property to ensure there are no hidden liabilities or issues that might affect your investment.

Risk Mitigation

Seasoned brokers are skilled in risk management. They can guide you in diversifying your tax lien investments across various properties, reducing the risk associated with a single property.

Redemption Assistance

When it comes to the point where you hold a tax lien on

a property, brokers can help navigate the process of property redemption or foreclosure. This is crucial for investors who may end up owning properties and need guidance on the next steps.

Tax lien investing is a unique and promising avenue for investors seeking high returns. However, the intricacies of local tax laws, property evaluation, and auction participation can make it a challenging endeavor. This is where tax lien brokers shine as indispensable guides in the journey of tax lien investments.

If you're intrigued by the idea of tax lien investing, enlisting the assistance of a knowledgeable tax lien broker could be your stepping stone to profitable property investments. With their expertise and guidance, you can navigate this intriguing asset class and potentially unlock the doors to a world of real estate opportunities.

Tax Liens Prospecting Niche Markets

Commercial Properties

When it comes to real estate investment, one avenue brimming with potential and profit is the world of commercial properties. This vast and dynamic sector encompasses a wide array of property types, from bustling office spaces in the heart of urban landscapes to sprawling industrial complexes on the outskirts of town. Commercial properties offer investors an opportunity to tap into the pulse of business and commerce, and in this article, we will explore the captivating world of commercial properties.

Diverse Opportunities Abound

The beauty of commercial properties lies in their diversity. Unlike the residential real estate market, where the main options revolve around homes, apartments, and condos, the commercial real estate landscape is rich with variety. From retail spaces to office buildings, industrial warehouses to hospitality establishments, the choices are endless.

One can choose to invest in a bustling shopping center with a mix of stores and restaurants, betting on the foot traffic generated by shoppers. Alternatively, you might consider an industrial property where manufacturers and logistics companies lease space for their operations. The options are as varied as your investment goals, making commercial properties an attractive playground for savvy investors.

Stability and Consistency

One of the key attractions of commercial properties is their potential for providing stable and consistent income streams. Commercial leases typically span several years, ensuring a reliable source of income for property owners. This predictability can be a significant advantage, especially for investors seeking to establish a steady financial foundation.

For example, a multi-tenant office building with long-term leases can offer an investor a dependable stream of rental income. In the ever-changing landscape of business, such stability can be invaluable, offering a sense of security and financial peace of mind.

Strategic Location Matters

The old adage in real estate, "location, location, location," is especially pertinent in the world of commercial properties. The success of a commercial property often hinges on its location, and investors must assess the potential of an area meticulously.

Proximity to highways, public transportation, and population centers can significantly impact the appeal of a commercial property. Accessibility to customers, clients, and employees is a critical factor. In bustling urban areas, commercial properties near central business districts may command high rental rates, while in suburban or rural settings, warehouses or industrial properties with room to expand may be the way to go.

Market Research and Due Diligence

In the realm of commercial real estate, knowledge is power. Successful investors dedicate time to thorough market research and due diligence. Understanding local economic trends, vacancy rates, and property values is vital. Moreover, evaluating the financial health of potential tenants and their ability to fulfill lease agreements is critical.

Investors often rely on market analysts, brokers, and real estate professionals to navigate the complexities of the commercial real estate market. These experts can provide insights into market dynamics, property valuation, and lease negotiations, making them valuable allies for investors looking to maximize their returns.

Adaptability to Economic Cycles

Commercial properties are often seen as a robust hedge against economic fluctuations. During economic upswings, demand for commercial spaces tends to rise as businesses expand. In contrast, during downturns, well-located and well-maintained properties are better equipped to weather the storm, as they are less susceptible to depreciation.

This adaptability is a significant advantage, as commercial properties can be part of a diversified investment portfolio. They offer investors the ability to balance the risks and rewards associated with real estate investments, making them a valuable tool for building long-term financial prosperity.

The world of commercial properties is teeming with opportunities and potential for investors. From diverse property types to consistent income streams and adaptability to economic cycles, it's an asset class that holds a special allure.

However, it's essential to approach commercial property investment with care, knowledge, and thorough research. Understanding the market, conducting due diligence, and seeking professional advice are all critical steps toward success.

Whether you're a seasoned investor or just embarking on your investment journey, the captivating world of commercial properties offers a wealth of opportunities for building a prosperous future. With the right strategy and a keen eye for potential, you can unlock the doors to financial success in this dynamic and ever-evolving sector of the real estate market.

Agricultural Tax Lien

Nestled in the heartland of our nation, away from the bustling city lights and towering skyscrapers, lies a treasure trove of investment opportunities largely overlooked by the average investor. These hidden gems are known as agricultural tax liens, a largely untapped resource in rural real estate.

The Allure of Agricultural Tax Liens

Agricultural tax liens represent an investment option that offers unique advantages, but are often obscured in the shadows of more glamorous investment choices. These liens are typically placed on properties when landowners fail to pay their property taxes. In return, investors have the opportunity to purchase these tax liens at a discounted rate, which can lead to substantial returns if the landowners fail to redeem them.

The Beauty of Rural Real Estate

The charm of rural real estate lies in its simplicity and natural beauty. These properties often consist of vast farmlands, ranches, or even open acreage, making them distinct from urban properties. Investing in agricultural land not only offers a piece of tranquility but also potential financial gains.

The Agricultural Tax Lien Process

The process of unearthing agricultural tax liens begins when landowners default on their property taxes, leaving municipalities in need of the unpaid funds to support local services and infrastructure. In response, local governments place tax liens on these properties, which can then be bought by investors at tax lien auctions.

The appeal for investors in these auctions is the potential for earning a hefty return. Upon purchasing the tax lien, the investor earns a fixed interest rate, which is typically higher than that of other traditional investments like stocks and bonds. Moreover, if the landowner fails to redeem the lien by paying the owed taxes with interest, the investor can acquire the property.

Why Agricultural Tax Liens Shine Bright

There are several factors that make agricultural tax liens shine brightly in the world of investment:

Steady Income: Investing in agricultural tax liens can provide a steady stream of income through the interest payments from delinquent property owners. This can serve as a consistent source of revenue for investors.

Secured Investment: Tax liens are backed by the property itself. If the landowner does not pay off the debt, the investor can gain possession of the property, making it a secured investment.

Diversification: Agricultural tax liens offer diversification. With a portfolio that includes a range of properties, investors can spread their risk, ensuring that a single property's performance does not have a disproportionate impact on their overall investment.

Long-Term Potential: Rural real estate often appreciates over time. As cities expand and demand for land increases, the value of rural properties can rise steadily.

Unveiling Hidden Opportunities

However, investing in agricultural tax liens is not without its challenges. Investors must be diligent in researching properties and understanding local regulations. Due diligence is crucial in uncovering hidden opportunities.

Navigating the world of agricultural tax liens requires patience, due diligence, and careful financial planning. Investors who take the time to uncover these hidden treasures in rural real estate can find a source of steady income and long-term growth potential. It's a world of investment that offers not only financial rewards but also a glimpse into the natural beauty and simplicity of rural life, all while securing your financial future. So, as you ponder your next investment, consider unearthing the hidden gem of agricultural tax liens, and you might find the buried treasure you've been searching for in rural America.

Sourcing Tax Lien is akin to a treasure hunt. With the strategies and insights provided, you have the map and tools to unearth these treasures. Remember that optimism in tax lien investing is not blind hope; it's the result of calculated decisions, informed choices, and well-devised strategies.

Envision yourself as an adventurer in the realm of Tax Lien, unearthing opportunities, and forging a path to financial prosperity. With the strategies for sourcing Tax Lien at your disposal, you're not just a passive investor; you're an active participant in a thriving market.

Identifying Promising Tax Lien Auctions

We unlock the door to identifying promising tax lien auctions, a journey brimming with potential and prosperity.

Tax Lien Auction Types

Now, the following are various types of tax lien auctions, each with its unique promise:

In-Person Auctions

In today's digital age, where the majority of our transactions occur through clicks and swipes, there's something incredibly exciting and nostalgic about in-person auctions. Stepping into an auction house, feeling the palpable anticipation in the air, and competing with fellow bidders with a simple nod or raise of your paddle – it's an experience like no other. In-person auctions are a captivating world that brings together the thrill of the hunt, the joy of discovery, and the excitement of competition.

The Allure of In-Person Auctions

Unveiling Hidden Treasures: When you attend an in-person auction, you're stepping into a realm of hidden treasures. These events are known for uncovering rare and unique items that have been tucked away in attics, basements, or private collections for years. From antique furniture to vintage memorabilia, you never know what gem you might stumble upon.
Live auctions often feature experts and appraisers who can provide valuable insights into the history and authenticity of items. You can ask questions, inspect items up close, and gain a deeper understanding of what you're bidding on.

In-person auctions are a multi-sensory experience. You can feel the texture of an antique rug, hear the echo of your fellow bidders, see the excitement in their eyes, and even catch a whiff of the timeworn leather of an old book. It's an immersion that transcends the limitations of online browsing.

There's nothing quite like the thrill of outbidding a fellow enthusiast. As the auctioneer's gavel strikes, the adrenaline surges. The competitive spirit and the pursuit of that perfect piece can turn an ordinary day into an extraordinary adventure.

Serendipity often plays a significant role in in-person auctions. You might arrive with a specific item in mind and leave with something entirely different – an unexpected treasure that you hadn't anticipated. These spontaneous finds are often the most cherished.

Attending live auctions allows you to connect with like-minded individuals who share your passion for collecting. Whether you're a seasoned collector or a novice, you can learn, share stories, and build relationships with fellow enthusiasts.

The Art of the Auction

Preparation: Before attending an in-person auction, do your research. Familiarize yourself with the items on offer, set a budget, and create a list of your top picks. Be prepared to inspect the items and ask questions if needed.

The Bidding Process: When it's time to bid, you'll often be given a numbered paddle. Raise it when you want to place a bid. Pay close attention to the auctioneer and the bidding increments. Know your limit, and don't get caught up in the heat of the moment.

Body Language: Observing the body language of your competitors can be a crucial advantage. A subtle nod or the twitch of an eyebrow can signal another bidder's intentions. The seasoned auction-goer knows how to read the room.

Etiquette: Auctions have their own unwritten rules of etiquette. Be respectful of fellow bidders, and don't bid if you're not genuinely interested in an item. Silence your cell phone and be attentive to the auctioneer.

In-person auctions offer a thrilling and immersive experience that cannot be replicated online. They are a voyage into the past, a treasure hunt in real-time, and a celebration of the art of the auction. Whether you're an avid collector or simply curious, attending an in-person auction is an adventure worth embarking on.

So, the next time you hear of an auction in your area, consider taking a step away from your digital devices and into the world of live bidding. Who knows, you might just walk away with a hidden treasure that will become a prized possession and a testament to your exciting journey through the world of in-person auctions.

Online Auctions

In a world where convenience is paramount, online auctions have emerged as a game-changer in the realm of retail therapy. The digital age has brought the excitement of traditional auctions right to your fingertips, and the concept is captivating the hearts and minds of millions. Whether you're a seasoned bargain hunter, a collector of rare items, or just someone looking for a thrilling shopping experience, online auctions are transforming the way we shop.

The Allure of Online Auctions

Picture this: You're comfortably seated on your sofa, armed with a cup of tea, a smartphone, and an irresistible urge to explore unique treasures. Welcome to the world of online auctions, where excitement meets convenience. Unlike traditional auctions that require your physical presence, online auctions offer a virtual front-row seat to a world of bidding wars and exclusive items. The allure lies in the simplicity and accessibility of the experience.

Diverse Offerings

One of the most captivating aspects of online auctions is the vast array of items up for grabs. From vintage jewelry and rare antiques to contemporary art and even cars, you can find virtually anything your heart desires. No longer limited to local offerings, these auctions connect you with sellers from around the world, expanding your shopping horizons like never before.

Bidding Wars: The Heart-Pounding Thrill

Auction houses often spark the competitive spirit within bidders, and online auctions are no exception. The thrill of watching the seconds tick away as you compete with others for your desired item is an experience that truly captivates. The adrenaline rush is addictive, making bidding wars as much a part of the appeal as the items themselves.

Treasure Hunt Vibes

Ever dream of discovering a hidden gem among the vast sea of listings? The world of online auctions is a treasure hunter's dream. A seemingly ordinary listing may turn out to be the rarest find, offering a sense of accomplishment that few other shopping experiences can rival. Scouring listings for that unique piece is a captivating adventure all its own.

Accessibility and Inclusivity

Online auctions have democratized the thrill of bidding. Whether you're a novice or a pro, the platforms are designed to be user-friendly and accessible to everyone. Inclusive by nature, they cater to a diverse audience, nurturing a global community of buyers and sellers.

Steeped in Tradition, Fueled by Technology

Online auctions have seamlessly married the traditions of classic auction houses with cutting-edge technology. The result is a captivating fusion that marries the old and the new. Expert auctioneers conduct events online, preserving the charm of a live auction while delivering it to your screens.

The Power of Knowledge

Online auctions empower bidders with detailed information about items, including their history, condition, and provenance. This insight transforms the experience into an educational journey. As you immerse yourself in the world of antiques, art, or collectibles, you become a more informed, discerning, and captivated consumer.

The Social Experience

In addition to the actual auctions, many online platforms offer opportunities to connect with like-minded enthusiasts. This social aspect adds another layer of fascination to the world of online bidding, as you share stories, tips, and insights with others who share your passion.

The Future of Shopping

As the digital landscape continues to evolve, online auctions are set to captivate even more shoppers. The convenience, diversity, and thrill they offer are undeniable. It's an exciting era for both buyers and sellers, and the future of shopping has never looked more captivating.

In the age of online auctions, the world is your marketplace, and your next prized possession is just a click away. So, get ready to be captivated, whether you're a seasoned bidder or a novice eager to embark on a thrilling shopping adventure.

Hybrid Auctions

What is a Hybrid Auction?

Hybrid auctions are a dynamic blend of the traditional and the digital. These auctions combine the excitement and atmosphere of a live, in-person auction with the convenience and global reach of online bidding. Think of it as the best of both worlds.

The concept is relatively simple but incredibly effective. Auction houses host physical events with an in-person auctioneer and audience, while simultaneously offering an online platform where bidders from across the globe can participate. In essence, the physical and virtual worlds merge seamlessly, allowing buyers and sellers to have the best of both realms.

The Best of Both Worlds

The Thrill of the Hammer: One of the unique aspects of a hybrid auction is the excitement it generates. The live audience creates an atmosphere charged with anticipation, reminiscent of the traditional auction experience. The sound of the hammer falling and the tension in the room are undeniable draws for many enthusiasts.

Global Accessibility: With hybrid auctions, geography is no longer a limiting factor. Bidders from different continents can compete for the same item, making it easier to connect buyers with rare or unique items. This expanded reach can be a game-changer for both sellers and collectors.

Convenience: For many, attending a physical auction can be time-consuming. Hybrid auctions allow buyers to participate from the comfort of their homes, cutting down on travel costs and time commitments.

Transparency: Transparency is vital in auctions, and the hybrid format enhances this. Buyers can see the live event, view items in real-time, and experience the auctioneer's chant, just like in a traditional setting.

Changing the Game

Hybrid auctions are changing the way the game is played. They are fostering a sense of inclusivity in a market that was once exclusive, allowing more people to participate and find that one-of-a-kind item. Whether you're a serious collector, a casual bidder, or someone looking to sell, the hybrid auction model offers something for everyone.

These auctions are also pushing the boundaries of what can be auctioned. While rare art and collectibles are still sought-after items, hybrid auctions are increasingly used to sell a broad range of products, from classic cars to real estate.

What Lies Ahead

The future of hybrid auctions is filled with exciting possibilities. As technology continues to advance, we can expect even more innovations in the auction world. Virtual reality auctions might become the norm, allowing bidders to explore items in a three-dimensional digital environment.

Additionally, blockchain technology is being explored to enhance the transparency and security of transactions in the auction world. With blockchain, the entire history of an item, from its creation to its auction record, can be tracked with precision.

Hybrid auctions are not just a temporary trend; they represent the future of buying and selling valuable items. They unite the charm of the traditional auction experience with the convenience and global reach of the digital age. It's a win-win for both buyers and sellers, and as technology continues to evolve, the world of hybrid auctions will only become more exciting and accessible. So, whether you're a collector seeking a rare gem or an enthusiast looking for a new hobby, consider exploring the electrifying world of hybrid auctions. You might just discover your next prized possession or an exciting way to diversify your assets.
Tax lien investing is a realm of endless opportunities, and your ability to identify the most promising auctions is your ticket to financial prosperity. Remember that optimism in this venture is not baseless; it's built on the foundation of knowledge and strategy.

As I always say, envision the opportunities that await you in the world of tax lien auctions. With the insights and criteria provided, you're not just an investor; you're an opportunist. Tax lien investing is about unlocking the potential within these auctions, seizing the opportunities they hold, and creating a brighter financial future.

Due Diligence and Property Research – Your Path to Success

Due diligence is the cornerstone of informed decision-making. It's the process of thoroughly investigating the properties you intend to invest in. In this chapter, we'll delve into the nuances of due diligence, ensuring that your investments are based on a strong foundation of research.

Property Ownership Research

Property ownership research is a powerful tool that empowers individuals, businesses, and investors to make informed decisions in the real estate world. In a market where property transactions involve significant financial investments, knowing the history, legalities, and ownership details of a property is paramount. This article explores the importance of property ownership research, how it works, and the benefits it offers to various stakeholders in the real estate landscape.

The Foundation of Informed Decisions

Property ownership research is essentially the process of delving into the background and history of a property to unearth vital information. This encompasses a wide range of details, from the current owner's identity and the property's transaction history to any legal encumbrances, liens, or past disputes associated with the property.

Why is this knowledge so crucial? Well, consider the purchase of a property, whether for personal residence, investment, or business purposes. Without adequate research, a buyer could unknowingly inherit a property with a cloudy legal history, such as unpaid property taxes or an unresolved boundary dispute. This could result in unexpected financial burdens and legal entanglements down the line.

Key Stakeholders and Their Needs

Property ownership research is invaluable for a variety of stakeholders in the real estate sector:

Homebuyers: For individuals looking to purchase a home, property ownership research ensures they are making a sound investment, free from legal disputes or hidden financial liabilities.

Real Estate Investors: Investors use this research to identify potential properties that promise high returns and low risks. Understanding a property's history is essential for making informed choices in a competitive market.

Real Estate Agents and Brokers: Agents and brokers rely on property ownership research to provide clients with transparent, trustworthy information, thereby building credibility and trust in their services.

Lenders and Financial Institutions: Banks and other lenders conduct ownership research to assess the property's value and assess its suitability as collateral for loans.

Legal Professionals: Lawyers involved in real estate transactions require thorough property ownership research to protect their clients' interests and navigate legal intricacies.

The Process of Property Ownership Research

Property ownership research involves a systematic exploration of various records and documents to build a comprehensive profile of a property. Some of the key steps include:

Public Records: This typically includes county or municipal records that detail property transactions, tax assessments, and ownership history. Researchers examine deeds, mortgages, and liens to understand the property's financial standing.

Land Surveys: Land surveys provide critical information about property boundaries, easements, and encroachments, helping to avoid boundary disputes.

Title Search: A title search is a fundamental aspect of property ownership research. It uncovers any outstanding legal issues, such as liens, judgments, or restrictions on the property title.

Property Tax Records: Property tax records indicate the financial health of a property and whether any taxes are overdue. They also highlight any changes in ownership.

Legal and Court Records: Researchers may delve into court records to uncover disputes or legal issues associated with the property.

Benefits of Property Ownership Research

Risk Mitigation: Property ownership research significantly reduces the risk of investing in a problematic property. By identifying any legal issues or financial burdens, investors can make informed decisions that protect their interests.

Increased Transparency: The transparency offered by ownership research builds trust among buyers, sellers, and real estate professionals, fostering a more reliable and ethical real estate market.

Financial Prudence: For those considering property purchases or investments, research ensures they are getting the best value for their money and not inheriting hidden financial burdens.

Legal Protection: Property ownership research can help protect against potential legal disputes, saving stakeholders significant time, money, and stress.

Property ownership research is an essential tool that empowers individuals, investors, and professionals to navigate the complex world of real estate with confidence. It provides transparency, mitigates risk, and ensures that the financial decisions made are grounded in reliable information.

In an ever-evolving real estate market, the knowledge gained from property ownership research is not just a competitive advantage; it's a necessity. Whether you're a first-time homebuyer, a seasoned investor, or a real estate professional, harnessing the power of research is the key to unlocking the full potential of your real estate endeavors.

Property Value Assessment

The world of real estate is like a complex puzzle, with each property representing a unique piece. When you think about investing in real estate or even just owning a home, one of the most fundamental aspects to understand is property value assessment. In essence, it's the art and science of determining how much a property is worth, and it plays a pivotal role in real estate transactions, investment decisions, and financial planning.

Property value assessment, also known as real estate appraisal, is the cornerstone of the entire real estate market. Whether you're a seasoned investor or a first-time homebuyer, unlocking the secrets of property value assessment can be your ticket to financial prosperity. So, let's dive into the fascinating world of real estate appraisal and explore why it matters.

The Essence of Property Value Assessment

At its core, property value assessment is the process of evaluating a property's monetary worth based on a variety of factors. These factors include location, size, condition, comparable properties, and market conditions. Appraisers, the professionals who perform property assessments, meticulously examine these variables to determine the fair market value of a property.

Fair market value is the price that a well-informed buyer is willing to pay and that a motivated seller is willing to accept in an open and competitive market. This valuation is not just a number; it's a reflection of a property's position in the ever-evolving real estate landscape.

Why Property Value Assessment Matters

Understanding property value assessment is crucial for several reasons:

1. Buying and Selling: For buyers and sellers, property value assessment sets the stage for negotiations. It helps sellers determine a reasonable asking price and provides buyers with assurance that they're making a fair purchase. If a property is priced too high or too low, it can lead to missed opportunities or financial loss.

2. Investment Decisions: Real estate investors rely on property value assessments to identify promising investment opportunities. By accurately gauging a property's worth, investors can decide whether to buy, sell, or hold a particular asset. It's the foundation for building a profitable real estate portfolio.

3. Financing: When you're seeking a mortgage to purchase a property, lenders will conduct their property value assessment to determine the loan amount. The lender wants to ensure that the property is valued at or above the loan amount. Knowing how properties are appraised can help borrowers present their case for loan approval.

4. Property Taxes: Local governments often use property value assessments to determine property taxes. Accurate assessments ensure that property owners pay their fair share of taxes, supporting public services like schools, infrastructure, and emergency services.

5. Wealth Management: For homeowners, understanding their property's value is a vital component of overall wealth management. The value of your home is a significant asset that can impact your net worth and financial planning, especially when considering retirement or estate planning.

The Art and Science of Appraisal

Property value assessment is a combination of art and science. While it involves objective data, such as square footage, the number of bedrooms, and the property's age, it also incorporates more subjective elements, like the property's overall condition, recent renovations, and neighborhood trends. Expert appraisers balance these factors to arrive at a precise valuation.

Appraisers use various methodologies to assess property value:

Sales Comparison Approach: This approach compares the subject property to similar properties that have recently sold in the area. It's especially useful for single-family homes.

Cost Approach: Appraisers determine the cost of replacing the property with a similar one, accounting for depreciation and market conditions. This method is valuable for newer properties and unique structures.

Income Approach: Typically used for income-producing properties like rental apartments, this method assesses a property's income potential.

Understanding these appraisal approaches empowers property owners, investors, and buyers to appreciate how appraisers arrive at their valuations.

Evolving with the Real Estate Landscape

The real estate market is dynamic, responding to economic trends, neighborhood developments, and societal shifts. Property value assessment is not a static process but rather one that evolves with the changing landscape. A property's value can increase with the growth of a thriving community or decrease due to economic downturns.

For homeowners and investors, keeping an eye on property values in their area and understanding the factors that drive changes is essential. It can guide decisions like renovations, selling, or capitalizing on the equity built in a property.

Bridging the Gap with Technology

In today's digital age, technology has transformed the property value assessment landscape. Online tools and databases provide real-time access to property information, historical data, and trends. These resources enable buyers, sellers, and investors to make more informed decisions.

Artificial intelligence and big data are also playing a role in property assessment. These technologies can analyze vast amounts of data to refine property valuations. With real-time updates and predictive analytics, they're becoming invaluable tools for those engaged in real estate.

The Future of Property Value Assessment

Property value assessment will remain a fundamental aspect of real estate for years to come. As technology and data analysis continue to advance, appraisals may become more accurate and accessible. Investors and homeowners will find themselves better equipped to make decisions that contribute to their financial success.

Whether you're purchasing your dream home, growing a real

estate portfolio, or simply staying informed about your assets, property value assessment is your compass in the world of real estate. Understanding its intricacies can be your key to unlocking the vast opportunities of the real estate market and building a secure financial future. So, embrace the art and science of property assessment, and let it guide you towards your real estate wealth.

Property Condition Analysis

When it comes to real estate, we've all heard the age-old mantra: location, location, location. But nestled within the very essence of a property's location lies another critical element that often goes unnoticed but is equally pivotal in determining its true value and potential – the property's condition.

Property condition analysis is the Sherlock Holmes of the real estate world. It scrutinizes every nook and cranny, inspects the walls for their whispered secrets, and deciphers the subtle clues embedded in every squeaky floorboard. In essence, it's the art and science of discovering a property's true identity.

The Silent Storytellers

Every property tells a story, and its condition is the storyteller. A weathered exterior may reveal battles fought with the elements, a creaky staircase might divulge the weight of countless footsteps, and a well-maintained garden could narrate a tale of a loving homeowner.

This silent narrative encompasses a wide range of aspects, including:

Structural Integrity: Is the property standing tall and strong, or are there signs of structural issues that may need expensive repairs?

Mechanical Systems: Are the heating, cooling, plumbing, and electrical systems in good working order, or are they time bombs ticking away?

Exterior and Roof: What's the state of the property's facade and roofing? Is water leaking in, or is the foundation secure?

Interior Features: How well are the interior components maintained? Are there signs of water damage, mold, or pest infestations?

Aesthetics: Are the aesthetics fresh and inviting, or is there a need for a renovation to breathe new life into the space?

The Quest for Value

Understanding a property's condition is not merely about the joy of discovery. It's a quest for value – value that could save you from a money pit or unearth a hidden gem. A thorough property condition analysis can lead to several benefits:

Informed Decision-Making: Knowing a property's true condition allows buyers to make informed decisions. It helps buyers gauge the potential costs of repairs or renovations and decide whether the investment aligns with their goals.

Negotiation Power: Armed with the knowledge of a property's condition, buyers can negotiate better deals. Sellers may be more willing to accommodate price adjustments or cover repair costs if issues are found.

Predict Future Expenses: For property owners, a detailed property condition analysis can help anticipate future maintenance and repair costs, allowing for more precise budgeting.

Assessing Investment Potential: Real estate investors rely heavily on property condition analysis to assess the potential for capital appreciation and rental income. A property in excellent condition often commands higher rental rates and property values.

The Tools of the Trade

Property condition analysis is not a task for the faint of heart. It requires a keen eye, a discerning mind, and sometimes, the assistance of professionals. Here are some tools that come into play:

Home Inspection: Home inspectors are like the detectives of property condition analysis. They delve into every aspect of the property, from the foundation to the roof, producing a comprehensive report.

Appraisals: Appraisers assess the value of a property by considering its condition and comparing it to similar properties in the area.

Engineering Reports: For a more in-depth look, especially at structural and mechanical systems, engineers might be brought in to provide detailed assessments.

Environmental Inspections: These inspections are crucial for uncovering potential hazards, like mold, lead paint, or asbestos.

Once you've unlocked the secrets that a property's condition holds, the next step is decision-making. This could be the purchase of a lifetime, an opportunity to transform a fixer-upper into a dream home, or a realization that it's best to walk away. Your newfound knowledge will be your guide.

Property condition analysis is an intricate journey, and it's not just for those well-versed in the intricacies of real estate. It's a tool for anyone seeking to buy, sell, or invest in property. It's a gateway to making sound financial decisions, based not just on a property's location but also on its deepest, most revealing whispers – its condition.

Legal Considerations

In our rapidly evolving world, understanding the legal landscape is more crucial than ever. Legal considerations touch every facet of our lives, from protecting our individual rights to shaping the dynamics of global business and society. In this article, we delve into the essential aspects of legal considerations, providing a comprehensive guide to help you navigate the complexities of the modern legal world.

Personal Legal Considerations

a. Civil Rights and Liberties: In a world deeply concerned with social justice and individual freedoms, it is vital to stay informed about your civil rights. This includes everything from freedom of speech, religion, and the press to the right to a fair trial.

b. Family Law: For families, legal considerations can range from marriage and divorce to child custody, alimony, and adoption. Understanding family law is essential for ensuring the well-being of your loved ones.

c. Estate Planning: Protecting your legacy through wills, trusts, and powers of attorney is a critical aspect of personal legal consideration. This safeguards your assets and ensures your wishes are honored.

Business Legal Considerations

a. Business Formation: If you're an entrepreneur or business owner, understanding the various business structures, such as sole proprietorships, partnerships, corporations, and LLCs, is crucial for setting up your enterprise effectively.

b. Intellectual Property: In our knowledge-driven economy, intellectual property laws play a vital role. Knowing how to protect your patents, trademarks, copyrights, and trade secrets is essential for preserving the fruits of your innovation.

c. Contracts and Agreements: The backbone of business relationships, contracts and agreements govern everything from employment terms to partnerships and mergers. Understanding these documents is vital to protect your interests.

Technology and Privacy

a. Cybersecurity and Data Protection: With the increasing frequency of cyberattacks and the vast amount of personal information stored online, knowledge of cybersecurity and data protection laws is essential for both individuals and businesses.

b. Digital Rights: As the digital world expands, it's essential to comprehend the legal aspects of digital rights, including net neutrality, freedom of speech online, and the protection of your personal data.

Environmental Law

a. Sustainability and Climate Change: With the world's growing focus on environmental preservation and the fight against climate change, understanding environmental laws is crucial. This includes regulations regarding emissions, clean energy, and conservation.

b. Natural Resource Management: Legal considerations in this area cover the responsible use of natural resources such as water, forests, and minerals, and the protection of endangered species and ecosystems.

International Law

a. Global Trade and Commerce: International business is subject to a complex web of trade agreements, sanctions, and treaties. Understanding international law is vital for businesses with global ambitions.

b. Human Rights and Refugees: The plight of refugees, human

trafficking, and international human rights issues require a global perspective and a grasp of international legal frameworks.

In our increasingly interconnected world, legal considerations have never been more relevant. Whether in your personal life or in business, understanding the legal landscape is essential for protecting your rights and interests. Laws continue to evolve, shaped by societal changes and technological advancements, making it imperative to stay informed.

Legal literacy is not limited to lawyers and legal professionals. It is a critical life skill that empowers individuals and businesses to navigate a complex world with confidence and competence. Stay curious, remain informed, and seek professional legal counsel when needed. With the right knowledge, you can harness the power of the law to protect your interests and contribute to a more just and equitable society.

How To Participate in Tax Lien Auctions for Profit

Before you set foot into the world of tax lien auctions, it's vital to understand the gateway to wealth that lies before you. Tax Lien are essentially legal claims placed on properties when owners fall behind on their property tax payments. When these Tax Lien are auctioned off, it is an opportunity for you to step in as the investor and essentially pay off the overdue taxes in exchange for the lien.

The real magic happens when the delinquent property owner, given a grace period determined by local laws, repays their overdue taxes with interest. This is where your gateway to wealth swings wide open. As the lienholder, you are entitled to the repayment of your investment along with the accrued interest. It's this interest that can transform tax lien investments into a lucrative venture.

The Thrill of Tax Lien Auctions

Participating in tax lien auctions is not merely an investment strategy; it's an exhilarating experience. Picture yourself seated among other investors in a crowded auction room or, in the digital age, joining an online auction from the comfort of your home. The excitement is palpable as you await your turn to bid on Tax Lien and seize an opportunity for substantial profit.

The thrill of tax lien auctions lies in the uncertainty, the opportunity to secure a property at a fraction of its market value. Imagine investing a relatively small sum and potentially acquiring a valuable piece of real estate. This scenario is not just plausible; it is the essence of tax lien auctions.

Untapped Potential of Distressed Properties

One of the most intriguing aspects of tax lien auctions is the opportunity they present with distressed properties. These are properties where owners, for various reasons, have been unable to keep up with their property tax payments. Distressed properties can range from vacant land to residential and commercial structures.

In the world of real estate, distressed properties are often diamonds in the rough. The key is to recognize the untapped potential within them. Tax lien auctions provide a gateway to acquire these properties and subsequently transform them into lucrative assets. This transformation might involve renovation, redevelopment, or even reselling the property at a higher value, creating substantial returns on your investment.

Building a Diverse Portfolio

Tax lien auctions offer an array of options for prospective investors. Whether you are looking for short-term gains or a long-term commitment, you can tailor your strategy to match your financial goals. The versatility of tax lien auctions allows you to build a diverse portfolio that can be customized to suit your preferences.

Your portfolio might include a mix of Tax Lien with varying interest rates, redemption periods, and property types. By diversifying your investments, you can minimize risks and maximize your potential for profit. This adaptability is one of the reasons tax lien auctions are considered a versatile and dynamic investment avenue.

The Power of Research and Due Diligence

While the idea of tax lien auctions sounds enticing, it is crucial to highlight the importance of research and due diligence. Like any investment, informed decisions are the pillars of success in the tax lien market. Before participating in an auction, take the time to thoroughly research the properties and Tax Lien available.

Understanding local laws, redemption periods, and the market value of properties is vital. It allows you to identify the properties with the most profit potential. Remember, not all Tax Lien will lead to foreclosure or redemption, so being discerning in your choices is crucial.

The Win-Win Scenario of Tax Lien

Tax lien auctions are a win-win scenario. They enable you to invest in properties and, in doing so, you assist local governments in recovering overdue taxes. As an investor, you are rewarded with potentially substantial returns on your investment, while the community benefits from the collection of unpaid property taxes.

The social impact of tax lien auctions is a noteworthy aspect of this investment avenue. By participating in these auctions, you are not only securing your financial future but also contributing to the economic well-being of the locality where the property is located.

Chapter 4 Understanding Tax Lien Certificates

Tax lien certificates represent a potent investment tool, capable of yielding substantial returns, diversifying investment portfolios, and providing a consistent income stream for investors. However, it is crucial to comprehend the nature and workings of tax lien certificates before delving into this investment avenue.

What exactly are tax lien certificates?

A tax lien certificate denotes a legal claim against a property on which property taxes have gone unpaid. When a property owner defaults on their property tax payments, the local government levies a tax lien against the property. If the property owner remains delinquent in their tax obligations, the government may opt to sell the tax lien certificate to an investor.

How do tax lien certificates operate?

When an investor acquires a tax lien certificate, they effectively extend a loan to the government. In return, the government disburses interest payments to the investor based on the delinquent tax amount. Moreover, the investor possesses the prerogative to initiate foreclosure proceedings on the property should the property owner fail to settle their overdue taxes.

Benefits of investing in tax lien certificates

There are a number of benefits to investing in tax lien certificates, including:

High returns: Tax lien investments can generate high returns, with some investors earning annual returns of 20% or more.

Steady stream of income: Tax lien investors typically receive a steady stream of income from interest payments and from foreclosing on properties and selling them.

Diversification: Tax Lien can help to diversify your portfolio, which can reduce your overall risk.

Tax advantages: Tax lien investors may be eligible for a number of tax advantages, such as the ability to deduct interest payments and the ability to defer capital gains taxes.

How to purchase tax lien certificates

Tax lien certificates are typically sold at tax lien auctions. Tax lien auctions are held by local governments to sell tax lien certificates to investors. To purchase a tax lien certificate, you will need to register with the local government that is holding the auction and deposit a cash deposit. Once you have registered and deposited a cash deposit, you will be able to bid on tax lien certificates at the auction.

Tips for investing in tax lien certificates.

Here are a few tips for investing in tax lien certificates:

Do your research. Before you bid on a tax lien certificate, it is important to research the property and the tax lien. This includes understanding the property's value, the amount of the tax lien, and the interest rate on the tax lien.

Bid strategically. Don't overpay for a tax lien certificate. Bid only what you are comfortable paying and what you think you can make a profit on.

Be prepared to foreclose. If the property owner does not pay the delinquent taxes, you may need to foreclose on the property and sell it to recoup your investment. Be prepared for this possibility.

Tax lien certificates can be a great way to generate high returns, diversify your portfolio, and create a steady stream of income. However, it is important to understand what tax lien certificates are and how they work before investing. Do your research, bid strategically, and be prepared to foreclose if necessary.

Imagine having the opportunity to generate high returns on your investment with relatively low risk. Imagine the opportunity to diversify your portfolio and to create a steady stream of income. Imagine the opportunity to help revitalize communities and provide affordable housing options.

All of this is possible by investing in tax lien certificates.

Tax lien certificates offer investors the opportunity to invest in property taxes and to generate high returns. Tax lien investments are also relatively low-risk, as investors have a secured interest in the property. Additionally, tax lien investments can help to diversify your portfolio and create a steady stream of income.

If you are looking for an investment opportunity that has the potential to improve your financial situation and to help you achieve your financial goals, I encourage you to consider investing in tax lien certificates.

Chapter 5: Winning at Tax Lien Auctions

Mastering the Auction Process

Pre-Auction Preparation

The world of real estate auctions is a thrilling place where opportunities to snag properties at a fraction of their market value abound. However, the path to auction victory isn't just about showing up and raising your bid paddle; it begins long before the auctioneer takes the stage. The secret to success lies in mastering the art of pre-auction preparation.

The Pre-Auction Advantage

A well-prepared bidder at a real estate auction is akin to a seasoned general entering a battlefield with a well-thought-out strategy. It's all about arming yourself with knowledge and resources that give you the upper hand. Here's how you can leverage pre-auction preparation to secure the property of your dreams and potentially save a substantial amount of money.

Research, Research, Research

Knowledge is your most potent weapon when it comes to real estate auctions. Begin by researching the property you're interested in and the neighborhood it's situated in. What's its current market value? Are there any outstanding liens or tax obligations? Is the property in good condition, or does it need extensive renovations? Is there a clear title? Understand the property inside and out.

Set Your Budget

Determine the maximum amount you're willing to bid. This should not be an arbitrary number but a well-considered budget that takes into account the property's potential purchase price, renovation costs (if any), and a buffer for unexpected expenses. Stick to this budget to avoid overextending yourself.

Visit the Property

Never buy a property sight unseen. Schedule a visit to the property to assess its condition. This firsthand inspection will help you identify any issues or opportunities and refine your budget accordingly.

Review Auction Terms

Each auction will have its terms and conditions, and it's essential to understand them thoroughly. These terms may include the deposit amount, bidding increments, the timeline for closing, and more. Ensure you're comfortable with these terms before participating in the auction.

Inspect Title and Liens

Have a title search conducted to uncover any existing liens, encumbrances, or legal issues related to the property. You don't want to inherit someone else's problems. Ensure the title is clear and can be transferred without complications.

Secure Financing

Get pre-approved for financing before the auction. This will help you understand your borrowing capacity and demonstrate your commitment to potential sellers. Pre-approval can be a deal-breaker in competitive auctions.

Attend Other Auctions

Consider attending other real estate auctions to get a feel for the process and practice your bidding strategy. While there, you might also find other properties that pique your interest.

Assemble Your Team

Real estate auctions can be complex, and having a team of experts in your corner can make all the difference. Consider working with a real estate agent, attorney, or a financial advisor with experience in real estate auctions.

Pre-auction preparation is the cornerstone of success in real estate auctions. By diligently researching, setting a clear budget, inspecting properties, and understanding the auction terms, you position yourself for a victorious bidding experience. Remember, preparation is the key to unlocking the hidden gems of the real estate market, and it can save you both time and money in the long run. So, equip yourself with knowledge, assemble your team, and embrace the excitement of real estate auctions with confidence. Your dream property might be just a well-prepared bid away.

Bidding Strategies

In the world of investment, successful bidding strategies can make the difference between financial triumph and disappointment. Whether you're navigating the intricate landscape of real estate auctions, stock markets, or even online marketplaces, mastering the art of bidding strategies is paramount. In this article, we delve into the intriguing world of bidding strategies, exploring the various techniques and insights that can help you gain an edge in the competitive realm of investments.

The Psychology of Bidding

Before we dive into the intricacies of bidding strategies, let's take a moment to understand the psychological underpinnings of this complex art. Bidding is not merely a transaction; it's a psychological battlefield. Bidders engage in a mental chess match, calculating their moves, reading their opponents, and strategizing their every bid.

The fear of missing out, known as FOMO, often influences bidding behaviors. It's a powerful motivator that can drive prices to unexpected heights. The thrill of competition and the desire to win can lead to emotional bidding, which might not always align with rational investment decisions. Recognizing these psychological factors is the first step in developing successful bidding strategies.

Auction Bidding Strategies

Sniping Strategy:

In online auctions or real estate bidding wars, the "sniping" strategy is a classic move. This technique involves waiting until the last possible moment to place a bid, catching other bidders off guard and leaving them with limited time to counter your offer.

This approach minimizes emotional bidding and often results in cost-effective wins.

Proxy Bidding:

In contrast to sniping, proxy bidding is an automated strategy that allows you to set your maximum bid. The platform will incrementally bid on your behalf until your limit is reached. Proxy bidding removes the need for constant monitoring and can be an effective way to secure an item or property without overpaying.

Early Bird Strategy:

The early bird strategy involves placing your bid as soon as the auction begins. This approach can send a strong signal to other bidders, establishing you as a serious contender. However, it also opens the door for counterbids, so use this strategy when you're confident in your valuation.

Stock Market Bidding Strategies

Limit Orders:

In the stock market, using limit orders can be a smart bidding strategy. With a limit order, you specify the price at which you are willing to buy or sell a stock. This approach allows you to set clear parameters and avoid emotional decision-making.

Dollar-Cost Averaging:

For long-term investors, dollar-cost averaging is an effective strategy. This method involves investing a fixed amount of money at regular intervals, regardless of the market's performance. Over time, this approach can lower your average purchase price and reduce the impact of market volatility.

Stop-Loss Orders:

When you want to protect your investments from sudden declines, stop-loss orders come to the rescue. This strategy enables you to set a predefined price at which you're willing to sell a stock to prevent further losses. It can be a valuable tool for risk management.

Real Estate Bidding Strategies

Know Your Budget:

Before engaging in real estate bidding, establish a clear budget. Knowing your financial limits prevents you from overbidding and making unwise investment decisions. Remember to account for additional costs like renovations, taxes, and fees.

Research and Due Diligence:

Thorough research and due diligence are vital. Understand the property's market value, its condition, and the neighborhood's potential for growth. Information is your greatest ally when formulating a bidding strategy.

Decisive Counteroffers:

When you face competing bids, your counteroffer should be prompt and decisive. Ambiguity can lead to losing opportunities. Respond to other bidders with confidence, and back up your offer with your research findings.

Bidding strategies are as diverse as the investment opportunities they relate to. Whether you're in the adrenaline-pumping world of auction houses, the dynamic stock market, or the ever-evolving real estate sector, mastering these strategies is the key to success.

To become a bidding strategist, remember to stay cool under pressure, base your decisions on research and data, and employ the right strategy at the right time. Understanding the psychology of bidding will help you anticipate your competitors and act strategically.

By embracing the art of bidding, you can open doors to opportunities, maximize returns, and ensure your investments align with your financial goals. So, when the gavel falls or the final stock bell rings, will you be the savvy strategist who secures victory?

Networking and Building Relationships

Optimism isn't limited to individual efforts; it's amplified by building a network of like-minded investors. We discuss the importance of networking and how it can open doors to opportunities you might never have encountered alone.

This segment is your passport to the thrilling world of tax lien auctions. The optimism that fuels your journey is a blend of preparation, strategy, and a profound understanding of the auction dynamics.

As you immerse yourself in the excitement of tax lien auctions, remember that your optimism is not merely a fleeting emotion. It's a product of your dedication to research, careful planning, and the strategies you employ. Your path to financial triumph is illuminated by this well-informed optimism.

The auctioneer's chant may be melodious, but it's your strategies and preparation that will be the sweetest sounds in your journey to prosperity. From mastering the auction process to understanding the risks and rewards, you're well on your way to claiming your place among successful tax lien investors.

Chapter 6: Acquiring Tax Lien with Confidence - Your Gateway to Financial Security

This chapter unveils the key to acquiring Tax Lien with confidence, setting you on a path to financial security and prosperity. Your confidence is your beacon in the complex world of tax lien investments, and here, we'll show you how to shine brightly.

The Core of Confidence

Confidence is the driving force behind successful tax lien investments. It's not about recklessness; it's about calculated decisions and informed choices. Chapter 6 is your guide to achieving this vital trait.

Confidence is not a product of ignorance; it's a result of diligence. Before acquiring Tax Lien, you must master the due diligence process, which ensures you invest wisely. In this chapter, we dive deep into the steps and strategies for thorough property research and evaluation.

The Psychology of Confidence

Confidence is not just about numbers and data; it's a psychological state of mind. We uncover the mindset and attributes that confident investors possess, including risk tolerance and the ability to adapt to changing circumstances.

Your financial security and prosperity hinge on the diligence, knowledge, and strategies you've acquired. Your success as a tax lien investor is an embodiment of the confidence you exude when making investment decisions.

Confidence is your currency in the world of tax lien investments. It's not just a feeling; it's a tangible asset that accumulates with every well-researched property, every auction you win, and every connection you make. As your confidence grows, so does your financial security.

Your path is illuminated by the knowledge you've acquired and the confidence that you now carry. So, step forward with certainty, for your gateway to financial security is wide open, and it's time to cross the threshold with unwavering confidence as your guiding light.

Chapter 7: Tax Lien Returns: Interest, Penalties, and Principal - Unveiling the Financial Powerhouse

We'll dive deep into the mechanics of returns, focusing on the triumvirate of interest, penalties, and principal.

Interest: The Engine of Profit

Interest: The Engine of Profit In the world of finance and investment, few forces are as powerful as the concept of interest. This seemingly small, unassuming word holds the key to unlocking financial growth, building fortunes, and ensuring the wheels of the economy keep turning. Interest, in all its forms, acts as the engine of profit, propelling individuals, businesses, and even entire nations toward prosperity. So, what is it about interest that makes it so vital? Why is it the linchpin of wealth creation and a cornerstone of modern economies? Let's delve into the captivating world of interest and explore how it powers the pursuit of profit.

The Foundation of Lending and Borrowing

At its core, interest is the cost of borrowing money. It's the compensation a lender receives for temporarily parting with their funds, trusting that it will be repaid along with a little extra. Borrowers, in turn, agree to pay interest for the privilege of accessing capital they don't possess at the moment. This simple but ingenious concept forms the bedrock of lending and borrowing, which, in turn, fuels economic activity.

Consider a scenario where someone wishes to buy a home but doesn't have the entire purchase price upfront. They turn to a bank for a mortgage loan. The bank agrees to lend the money, but in exchange, the borrower will pay back the principal amount (the original loan) plus interest over a specified period. This interest is the reward for the bank's trust and the compensation for the delay in accessing its own capital.

Investment and Returns

Interest doesn't just benefit lenders; it also entices investors. It's the reason individuals entrust their hard-earned money to banks, bonds, or savings accounts. It's the catalyst behind entrepreneurs seeking capital for their ventures. Interest, in the context of investments, represents the potential for growth.

When you deposit money in a savings account, the bank pays you interest for the privilege of using your funds. The longer your money remains in the account, the more interest it accrues. This incentivizes saving and allows your wealth to grow passively. It's a modest but reliable form of investment.

Entrepreneurs and businesses often rely on loans or investors to finance their growth. Investors, whether individual or institutional, provide capital in exchange for interest payments. The prospect of earning a return on their investments motivates these financial backers. It's not just a loan; it's an opportunity to generate profit through interest.

The Magic of Compound Interest

If simple interest is the foundation, compound interest is the skyscraper of financial success. Compound interest is interest calculated on both the initial principal and the accumulated interest from previous periods. It's the magical force that multiplies wealth exponentially over time.

Imagine investing $1,000 in a savings account with a 5% annual interest rate. At the end of the first year, you earn $50 in interest, bringing your total to $1,050. Now, in the second year, the interest is calculated not just on the initial $1,000 but also on the $50 you've earned. This compounding effect continues, year after year, magnifying your wealth. Over time, it transforms a modest investment into a substantial nest egg.

From Personal Finances to Global Economics

Interest extends beyond the individual and family level. It's a driving force in global economies. Central banks use interest rates to regulate economic activity. Lowering interest rates stimulates borrowing and spending, which can boost economic growth. Conversely, raising interest rates can cool down an overheated economy, curbing inflation.

National governments issue bonds to raise capital, paying interest to bondholders. This enables governments to finance infrastructure projects, healthcare, education, and other essential services. Investors purchase these bonds with the expectation of earning interest, contributing to the nation's development.

Interest, the Lifeline of Profit

In the world of finance, interest is the lifeline of profit. It's the spark that ignites savings and investments, the catalyst that drives lending and borrowing, and the secret sauce behind long-term wealth accumulation. Whether you're an individual aiming to grow your savings or a global economy navigating financial stability, interest is the engine that keeps the wheels of prosperity turning.

So, next time you hear the word "interest," remember that it's not just a rate or a percentage. It's the powerhouse that shapes the financial landscapes of individuals, businesses, and nations, driving them toward profit, progress, and prosperity.

Penalties: The Catalyst of Returns

Investing often conjures images of gains and profits, but what about the often-overlooked component that fuels returns—penalties? While penalties are typically associated with financial setbacks, they can paradoxically serve as catalysts for remarkable returns when approached strategically.

Redefining Penalties

Before delving into how penalties can boost returns, it's essential to redefine our perception of them. Penalties aren't just financial punishments; they can also be viewed as incentives for prudent decision-making.

Consider, for instance, the world of tax lien investing. Property owners who fall behind on their taxes face penalties. However, these financial penalties can create a unique investment opportunity, turning delinquent taxes into a pathway for investors to achieve remarkable returns.

The Tax Lien Paradox

Tax lien investing centers on the mechanism that municipalities employ to recoup unpaid property taxes. When a property owner falls behind on tax payments, the local government places a lien on the property. This lien includes the outstanding taxes, and, importantly, penalties or interest charges.

These penalties accrue over time, and this is where the opportunity arises. Investors can purchase these liens from the local government, essentially lending money to cover the unpaid taxes. In return, they receive the right to collect the overdue taxes, plus the penalties, from the property owner.

The Power of Compound Interest

Penalties can become a catalyst for impressive returns due to the magic of compound interest. Compound interest is interest that accrues on both the principal (the original amount of money) and any interest that has previously been added to the principal. Over time, compound interest can dramatically increase the overall return on investment.

In the context of tax lien investing, the longer the property owner delays paying their taxes, the more significant the penalties grow. When they eventually settle their debt, they not only repay the original amount but also the substantial penalties that have accrued. This can lead to returns that significantly outpace traditional investment options.

Risk and Reward

Like any investment, tax lien investing carries its share of risks. Property owners may fail to redeem the lien, leading to foreclosure. However, this potential downside is balanced by the significant upside potential. By carefully selecting tax liens and properties, investors can mitigate risks while maximizing returns.

Beyond Tax Liens

While tax lien investing is a prominent example of how penalties can catalyze returns, this principle can be applied to other areas of investment. Early withdrawal penalties from retirement accounts or certificates of deposit can serve as motivators for long-term investing, potentially leading to substantial returns down the road.

Penalties may have a reputation for causing financial headaches, but they can also serve as powerful catalysts for returns when approached strategically. Tax lien investing showcases how penalties, when managed effectively, can transform into a lucrative investment opportunity.

In the world of finance, it's essential to look beyond the surface, recognizing the hidden potential in every financial transaction. Penalties, traditionally viewed as setbacks, can become the driving force behind remarkable returns, highlighting the inherent beauty of the financial world's intricacies.

Principal: Your Ticket to Property Ownership

In the world of finance and real estate, "principal" is a term that holds a special place. It's not just a word; it's the cornerstone upon which your path to property ownership is built. So, what exactly is principal? In the realm of property ownership, principal refers to the amount of money you initially invest or borrow to acquire a property. This amount forms the basis for your property ownership journey.

The Homebuyer's Ladder

Imagine you're a first-time homebuyer. You've saved diligently, found the perfect property, and are now seeking a mortgage to turn your homeownership dream into reality. Here's how principal fits into this picture:

Down Payment: Your principal starts with the down payment. This is the initial amount you pay from your own savings. It's your commitment to the property, and it demonstrates your intent to own it. The larger your down payment, the smaller the principal you'll need to borrow through a mortgage.

Mortgage Principal: The remainder of your property's purchase price is typically covered by a mortgage. This is where the concept of "mortgage principal" comes into play. Your monthly mortgage payments are split into two parts: one portion goes toward paying down the principal, reducing your initial debt, and the other part is the interest you owe to the lender.

Why Principal Matters

Now that you understand what principal is, let's delve into why it's so crucial:

Equity Growth: Every payment you make toward the mortgage principal increases your ownership stake in the property. As you gradually reduce the principal balance, you're essentially growing your equity in the property. This equity can be tapped into later for various financial needs.

Shorter Loan Terms: If your financial situation allows, you can make additional principal payments. This accelerates the reduction of your loan balance, allowing you to pay off your mortgage earlier. A shorter loan term not only saves you money on interest but also leads to full property ownership sooner.

Financial Flexibility: Understanding and managing your principal allows you to take control of your financial future. You can choose to refinance, take out home equity loans, or use your property's equity for investment opportunities or home improvements.

Building Your Property Legacy

Principal isn't just about numbers; it's about making your dreams come true. It's about planting the seeds of property ownership, nurturing them through consistent payments, and eventually reaping the rewards of homeownership. It's about having a place to call your own, where you create memories and build your legacy.

Principal is your ticket to property ownership, and it's a journey worth embarking on. So, whether you're a first-time homebuyer or a seasoned property owner, remember that principal is the key to transforming a house into a home and an investment into a legacy.

The world of tax lien returns is not just about numbers; it's a realm of financial opportunities waiting to be seized. This chapter empowers you to make the most of those opportunities, amplifying your financial prosperity and opening doors to a brighter financial future.

Your confidence will be unwavering as you grasp the intricacies of interest, penalties, and principal. With each piece of knowledge, you're one step closer to financial independence and success. Chapter 6 is your guide, your mentor, and your key to maximizing your tax lien investment returns, setting you on a path to financial prosperity that knows no bounds.

Chapter 8: Dealing with Non-Payment - Navigating Challenges with Confidence

Non-Payment in Tax Lien Investments

Tax lien investments have gained popularity among savvy investors seeking opportunities to diversify their portfolios and earn high returns. While this asset class can indeed be lucrative, it's essential to understand and prepare for the risks associated with it. One such risk is non-payment, where property owners fail to redeem their tax liens. In this article, we will delve into the world of non-payment in tax lien investments, exploring the challenges it poses and the opportunities it may bring.

Non-Payment Scenarios

Non-payment occurs when property owners fail to redeem their tax lien certificates by settling their outstanding taxes. In this situation, investors may face challenges, but there are also opportunities to explore.

Challenges of Non-Payment

Delayed Returns: Non-payment can delay your expected returns on the investment. It means you may not receive your principal amount back with the anticipated interest as quickly as you had hoped.

Potential Legal Procedures: In some cases, dealing with non-payment may involve legal proceedings, which can be both time-consuming and costly. This is a downside to consider.

Opportunity Cost: Your capital may be tied up in a non-performing asset, potentially limiting your ability to invest elsewhere during this time.

Opportunities in Non-Payment

Higher Interest Accrual: When property owners fail to redeem their tax lien certificates promptly, the interest continues to accrue, often at a high fixed rate. This means your eventual return could be higher than initially anticipated.

Property Acquisition: In the event of non-payment, you may have the opportunity to foreclose on the property and take ownership. You can either sell it or potentially rent it out, turning the property into a source of income.

Portfolio Diversification: Non-payment, while posing challenges, can also offer an opportunity to diversify your investment portfolio. You can explore various options, such as trading the lien with another investor or investing in different types of tax liens or assets.

Navigating Non-Payment

Here are some strategies for navigating non-payment in tax lien investments:

1. Due Diligence: Before investing, conduct thorough research on the properties you're considering. Assess the potential risks and rewards, and consider the likelihood of non-payment.

2. Risk Management: Diversify your tax lien portfolio to spread risk. Consider investing in various property types and regions to minimize the impact of non-payment on your overall investments.

3. Legal Expertise: If you encounter non-payment, it may be wise to consult with legal professionals who specialize in tax lien investments. They can guide you through the process of resolving non-payment issues, potentially accelerating the resolution.

4. Patience: Tax lien investments are typically long-term, and non-payment can be part of the journey. Exercise patience and allow the process to unfold.

Non-payment is a challenge that tax lien investors may face, but it's important to recognize that it's not the end of the road. It's an aspect of the investment process that, with careful planning and strategy, can be managed effectively. While non-payment may delay returns, it can also lead to higher interest accrual and property acquisition opportunities. Successful tax lien investors approach non-payment with due diligence, risk management, legal expertise, and patience.

In the world of investments, challenges often come hand in hand with opportunities. Navigating non-payment in tax lien investments can be a rewarding experience for those who are prepared and well-informed. It's a reminder that, in the realm of finance, adaptability and strategic thinking are key to achieving your investment goals.

The Power of Patience: Extending the Redemption Period

The Power of Patience

Let's explore why patience is an invaluable asset in the world of tax lien investments:

Extended Redemption Periods Mean Bigger Returns: In the world of tax lien investing, time is money. When the redemption period is longer, investors have more time for their investments to mature. This extended period allows more interest to accrue on the tax lien, translating into larger returns when the property is eventually foreclosed.

Safeguard Against Impulsive Decisions: Investors who lack patience may rush into hasty decisions, potentially selling tax liens at a discount or making impulsive decisions that don't align with their long-term goals. By embracing patience, investors can stay the course and wait for the right moment to maximize their returns.

Protection Against Market Fluctuations: Markets are known to ebb and flow. By patiently holding onto tax liens, investors can weather market fluctuations and wait for optimal market conditions to foreclose on a property or sell their tax liens. This resilience can lead to more substantial profits.

Steady Income Streams: Properties in the tax lien process often require time to turn around, repair, or sell. During this period, investors can enjoy a steady stream of income generated by the interest on their tax liens, supplementing their cash flow and increasing their financial stability.

Maximizing the Power of Patience

To fully harness the power of patience in tax lien investments, consider these strategies:

Diversify Your Portfolio: Diversifying your investments across various tax liens with different redemption periods can help balance your portfolio and ensure a steady income stream.

Continuous Learning: Educate yourself about tax lien laws and market trends. Stay informed about the properties you invest in and any potential changes that may affect their redemption periods.

Clear Risk Management: Implement risk management strategies to safeguard your investments during extended redemption periods, and set predefined limits to manage potential downsides.

Be Adaptable: Adapt your strategy as market conditions change. The ability to shift your approach in response to new information or opportunities is key to successful tax lien investments.

A Patient Path to Prosperity

In the fast-paced world of investments, the power of patience stands out as a key driver of success in tax lien investing. By embracing extended redemption periods, investors can maximize their returns, make informed decisions, and create a resilient investment strategy. The value of patience extends far beyond the tax lien arena, as it is a fundamental element in crafting a successful investment journey. As the saying goes, "Patience is bitter, but its fruit is sweet." In the world of tax lien investments, the sweetness of patience often leads to a harvest of prosperity and financial success.

Foreclosure

Foreclosure often carries a negative connotation, conjuring images of financial hardship and property losses. However, there's another side to this story that many prospective homebuyers and investors have yet to discover. For those who understand the intricacies of foreclosure, it can be a unique and exciting pathway to property ownership.

The Foreclosure Dilemma

Foreclosure occurs when a homeowner is no longer able to meet their mortgage payments, leading to the lender taking control of the property to recover the debt. It is undoubtedly a distressing time for the homeowner, but it's also a significant opportunity for others.

Foreclosed Properties: A Hidden Treasure Trove

For savvy buyers, foreclosed properties represent a treasure trove of opportunities. Here's why:

Discounted Prices: One of the most compelling reasons to consider foreclosures is the potential for significant savings. Lenders are primarily interested in recovering their investment, so foreclosed properties are often priced well below market value.

Diverse Property Types: Foreclosures come in all shapes and sizes, from single-family homes and condos to commercial properties. This diversity allows buyers to find a property that suits their needs and goals.

Investment Potential: Real estate investors often find foreclosed properties to be excellent investments. With a well-chosen property and some renovation work, investors can turn a foreclosed house into a valuable income-generating asset.

How to Get Started with Foreclosure

If you're interested in exploring the world of foreclosure, here's a step-by-step guide to help you get started:

Research: Begin by researching the foreclosure process in your area. Familiarize yourself with local laws and regulations.

Budget and Financing: Determine your budget and secure your financing. Knowing how much you can spend will help narrow down your options.

Work with a Real Estate Agent: Engage a real estate agent who specializes in foreclosures. They can help you locate suitable properties and navigate the intricacies of the buying process.

Property Inspection: Always conduct a thorough property inspection. Foreclosed homes may require repairs, so it's essential to know what you're getting into.

Bid at Auctions: Many foreclosures are sold at auctions. Participating in these auctions can be a thrilling way to acquire a property.

Legal Assistance: It's advisable to consult an attorney experienced in foreclosure laws to ensure a smooth and legally compliant purchase.

Foreclosure Challenges to Keep in Mind

While the path to property ownership through foreclosure offers great potential, there are challenges to consider:

Competitive Market: Due to the attractive pricing, the competition for foreclosed properties can be fierce. Be prepared for bidding wars.

Property Condition: Many foreclosed properties are sold "as-is," which means they may require extensive repairs.

Hidden Liabilities: There could be liens or legal issues attached to the property that the buyer may inherit.

Foreclosure represents an intriguing journey to property ownership, offering both substantial savings and potential financial rewards. However, it is not without its risks, and it's vital to approach the process with careful planning, thorough research, and professional guidance.

For those willing to navigate the complexities of foreclosure, it can be a path that leads to fulfilling the dream of property ownership or creating an exciting real estate investment portfolio. As with any financial endeavor, knowledge is the key to success, and understanding the intricacies of foreclosure is your stepping stone to a brighter property-owning future.

Turning Challenges into Opportunities

Non-payment doesn't have to be a stumbling block; it can be a stepping stone to your financial success. This chapter will empower you to face challenges head-on, with the knowledge and confidence required to overcome them. With each solution presented, your confidence will grow, and your journey in tax lien investments will become smoother and more prosperous.

Your unwavering confidence in dealing with non-payment is not just an attribute; it's a skill that will set you apart as a successful tax lien investor. By the end of this chapter, you'll possess the tools, strategies, and knowledge to navigate the complex terrain of non-payment and transform it into an opportunity for financial growth and prosperity.

Non-payment is an inevitable part of the tax lien investment landscape, but it's crucial to understand that it's not the end of the road; it's a fork in the journey. The first step in effectively handling non-payment is acknowledging that it can happen for various reasons, and it's your preparedness and strategy that will make all the difference.

Mitigating Risks and Losses: Your Shield in Tax Lien Investing

While tax lien investing promises a multitude of financial rewards, it's essential to be equipped with strategies to mitigate potential pitfalls and safeguard your investments.

The Inevitability of Risks

Before we delve into the strategies to mitigate risks and losses, it's important to recognize that no investment comes without risks. Tax lien investing is no exception. These risks could stem from the property's condition, the financial stability of the property owner, or even external economic factors. However, understanding that risks exist is the first step towards managing and mitigating them.

Risk Assessment and Mitigation

This segment will walk you through the process of risk assessment, which involves identifying and evaluating the potential risks associated with your tax lien investments. Through real-life examples and case studies, you will learn how to effectively assess the risks involved in different investment scenarios. This understanding is pivotal in the creation of a robust risk mitigation strategy.

Diversification: The Key to Risk Management

Diversification is a proven strategy in the world of investments, and it is no different for tax lien investments. This chapter provides insights into diversifying your portfolio effectively. By spreading your investments across a variety of Tax Lien, you can minimize the impact of a poor-performing property and ensure a balanced risk exposure.

Insurance: A Safety Net for Investors

While not always utilized in tax lien investing, insurance can be a useful safety net to mitigate risks and potential losses. This chapter explores the types of insurance that can benefit tax lien investors and how to choose the right policies. Knowing that you have insurance coverage in place can provide peace of mind in your investment journey.

Building a Resilient Investment Portfolio

Ultimately, you are encouraged to build a resilient investment portfolio that can withstand unexpected challenges. With the strategies, tools, and knowledge gained from this chapter, you'll be better prepared to mitigate risks and minimize losses. While no investment is entirely risk-free, the ability to manage and reduce risks is within your control.

Chapter 9 The Tax Deed Option in Tax Lien Investing

Key Differences Between Liens and Deeds

In the world of real estate, liens and deeds are two important legal documents that define property ownership and rights. While they are often used interchangeably, there are some key differences between the two.

Imagine being able to purchase a property at a fraction of its market value, simply because the previous owner failed to pay their property taxes. That is the power of tax lien investing.

Of course, no investment is without risk. But with careful planning and execution, you can minimize your risk and maximize your chances of success.

If you are looking for an investment opportunity that has the potential to change your life, tax lien investing is worth considering. With the right knowledge and strategy, you can generate high returns, build wealth, and achieve your financial goals.

What is a Tax Deed?

A tax deed is a legal document that transfers ownership of a property from the government to a new owner. Tax deeds are issued when the property owner fails to pay their property taxes. The government can then foreclose on the property and sell it to satisfy the debt.

Investors can purchase tax deeds at auction. If the investor is the winning bidder, they will receive a tax deed and become the new owner of the property.

Risks of Tax Deed Investing

Here are some of the risks of tax deed investing:

Redemption: The property owner may redeem the tax deed before the foreclosure process is complete. This means that the investor will lose their investment.

Title issues: The property may have title issues, such as liens or easements. These title issues can make it difficult to sell the property or to obtain a mortgage.

Occupancy issues: The property may be occupied by the previous owner or by tenants. It can be expensive and time-consuming to evict occupants from a property.

Condition of the property: The property may be in poor condition and require repairs. This can add to the investor's costs.

Rewards of Tax Deed Investing

Here are some of the rewards of tax deed investing:

High returns: Tax deed investors can generate high returns on their investment. Some investors have reported earning returns of 20% or more.

Leverage: Tax deed investors can use leverage to purchase properties that they would not be able to afford to purchase outright. This can amplify their returns.

Appreciation: The value of real estate can appreciate over time. This means that tax deed investors may be able to sell the properties they purchase for a profit, even if they do not generate any income from the properties.

How to Mitigate the Risks of Tax Deed Investing

To mitigate the risks associated with tax deed investing, there are several steps you can take:

Thoroughly research the property: Before acquiring a tax deed, conduct a comprehensive investigation into the property. This should include identifying potential title and occupancy issues, as well as inspecting the property to assess its condition.

Opt for tax deeds with high interest rates: Choosing tax deeds with elevated interest rates will help maximize your return on investment.

Focus on tax deeds for properties with substantial equity: This strategy reduces your risk of loss in case the property owner redeems the tax deed.

Collaborate with a qualified tax deed advisor: A knowledgeable tax deed advisor can assist in pinpointing sound investment opportunities and guide you through the tax deed process effectively.

Now, let's explore ways to maximize your tax deed investment returns:

Purchase tax deeds at auction: Acquiring tax deeds through auctions is the most cost-effective approach.

Hold onto tax deeds until maturity: By retaining tax deeds until they mature, you can accrue interest on your investment over time.

Target buyers interested in fix-and-flip properties: These buyers are typically willing to pay a premium for tax deeds, enhancing your potential returns.

Consider partnerships with other investors: Collaborating with fellow investors allows you to pool resources and collectively invest in larger properties.

In summary, strategic research, wise choices in tax deed selection, and effective investment tactics can significantly impact the success of your tax deed investments.

Tax deed investing can be a great way to generate high returns with relatively low risk. However, it is important to understand the risks involved and to develop a sound investment strategy before investing in tax deeds. By following the tips above, you can mitigate the risks and maximize your chances of success.

Furthermore, Tax deed investing is one of the most exciting and rewarding investment opportunities available today. With the right knowledge and strategy, you can generate high returns with relatively low risk.

Imagine being able to purchase a property at a fraction of its market value, simply because the previous owner failed to pay their property taxes. That is the power of tax deed investing.

Of course, no investment is without risk. But with careful planning and execution, you can minimize your risk and maximize your chances of success.

If you are looking for an investment opportunity that has the potential to change your life, tax deed investing is worth considering. With the right knowledge and strategy, you can generate high returns, build wealth, and achieve your financial goals.

Characteristic	Lien	Deed
Purpose	To secure a debt	To transfer ownership
Priority	Liens typically have priority over deeds	Deeds typically have priority over liens
Transferability	Liens can be transferred to new owners	Deeds can only be transferred by the current owner
Effect on ownership	Liens do not affect ownership	Deeds transfer ownership

The following table summarizes the key differences between liens and deeds:

Chapter 10: Why Tax Lien is a Wealth-Building Strategy

Low Entry Barriers

In the world of investment, there exists a spectrum that stretches from the risk-averse to the thrill-seeking, from the conservative to the daring. Somewhere within this spectrum lies a sweet spot for individuals who are in pursuit of the elusive balance between risk and reward. This article delves into a niche investment strategy where low entry barriers meet high potential rewards: tax lien investing.

Picture this: you're seeking an investment opportunity that doesn't demand a fortune as a down payment, doesn't require in-depth knowledge of complex financial instruments, and yet offers the potential for substantial financial gain. If this sounds appealing, then tax lien investing might be your ticket to the world of investment success.

Demystifying Tax Lien Investing

Before we explore the enticing aspects of low entry barriers and high potential rewards, let's demystify the core concept of tax lien investing. Tax lien investing hinges on one fundamental principle: local governments need your help to ensure the smooth running of their essential services. To guarantee that property taxes are paid promptly, governments often resort to issuing tax liens on properties where the owners have fallen behind on their tax payments.

A tax lien certificate, representing the amount of delinquent taxes plus interest, is offered for sale to investors at a public auction. This marks the starting point of your journey into tax lien investing. Acquiring a tax lien certificate means you're stepping into the shoes of the local government as the tax collector. This certificate grants you the legal claim to the property, should the owner fail to settle their debts.

Here's the beauty of tax lien investing: it's one of the most accessible investments for a wide range of investors. Whether you're a seasoned financial guru or someone just dipping their toes into the vast ocean of investing, the barriers to entry are refreshingly low.

Minimal Capital: You don't need a substantial sum of money to start tax lien investing. In many cases, you can participate in tax lien auctions with a modest amount. This low capital requirement opens doors for those who might not have deep pockets to dive into traditional investments like real estate or the stock market.

Knowledge Accessibility: You don't have to be a finance expert to start. Basic research and a fundamental understanding of local tax laws are often sufficient to make informed investment decisions. Plenty of resources, books, and online forums are available to educate and guide newcomers.

No Need for Complex Instruments: Tax lien investing is straightforward. You invest in a tax lien certificate, and your potential returns come from the interest on the delinquent taxes or property ownership in case of default. You don't need to navigate a complex maze of financial instruments.

High Potential Rewards

The appeal of tax lien investing isn't just its low entry barriers but also the tantalizing potential rewards it offers:

High Returns: One of the primary attractions of tax lien investing is the potential for substantial returns. The interest rates on delinquent taxes can soar into the double digits in many cases. This means your initial investment can grow significantly over time.

Steady Income Stream: For those seeking a reliable income source, tax lien investing can provide a steady stream of interest payments. This regular income can help you supplement your existing earnings or build a nest egg for the future.

Diversification: Diversifying your investment portfolio is a smart strategy to manage risk. Tax lien investing offers an opportunity to diversify your assets, reducing your exposure to fluctuations in traditional markets like stocks or real estate.

A World of Potential Awaits

In the world of investment, the confluence of low entry barriers and high potential rewards is a rare occurrence. Tax lien investing stands out as a viable avenue for both novice and experienced investors. The simplicity of the process, combined with the exciting potential for financial growth, makes it an alluring option for those seeking to make their money work for them.

While tax lien investing carries a level of risk, the rewards it can yield are more than enticing. Whether you're looking to generate high returns, create a reliable income stream, or diversify your investment portfolio, tax lien investing has the potential to unlock the world of opportunity. It's a world where low entry barriers lead to high potential rewards, and the journey is as rewarding as the destination.

Guaranteed Returns

In the world of finance, where unpredictability often reigns supreme, the phrase "guaranteed returns" shines like a beacon of financial security. It conjures images of a surefire path to prosperity, offering investors the promise of their investments flourishing, no matter the market's capricious fluctuations. But what do guaranteed returns really mean, and how can you harness this financial promise to secure your financial future?

Defining Guaranteed Returns

At its core, guaranteed returns represent an investment scenario in which the principal amount you invest is safeguarded from any loss, and a predetermined interest rate or return is provided by the issuer, typically over a specific period. This essentially means that, regardless of market volatility or economic turbulence, your initial investment remains intact, and you are assured of earning the stated interest.

Guaranteed returns are often offered through various financial instruments, including certificates of deposit (CDs), fixed annuities, government bonds, and certain insurance products. While the specific terms and rates may vary between these instruments, the common thread is the assurance of stability and the peace of mind that your money is not subject to market risks.

The Appeal of Guaranteed Returns

The allure of guaranteed returns is undeniable, especially in an era when uncertainty seems to be the only certainty. Here are some reasons why investors are drawn to this financial haven:

1. Risk Mitigation: In a world where financial markets can plummet overnight and economic conditions remain unpredictable, investors seek ways to mitigate risk. Guaranteed returns provide a shield against market volatility, offering the comfort of a secure financial future.

2. Reliable Income: For retirees or individuals seeking a steady income stream, guaranteed returns offer a reliable source of funds. This financial predictability is invaluable for covering living expenses, particularly in one's golden years.

3. Principle Preservation: The fear of losing hard-earned money in turbulent markets can keep many investors up at night. With guaranteed returns, the initial investment is protected, ensuring that your wealth remains intact.

4. Diversification: Investors often seek to diversify their portfolios to manage risk. Including guaranteed return investments adds a layer of stability, creating a balanced mix of risk and security in their financial strategy.

5. Long-Term Planning: For those with specific long-term goals, such as purchasing a home, funding a child's education, or securing a comfortable retirement, guaranteed returns can be a fundamental building block of their financial plan.

Types of Guaranteed Return Investments

Several investment vehicles offer guaranteed returns:

1. Certificates of Deposit (CDs): These are time deposits offered

by banks and credit unions. CDs typically have fixed terms and interest rates. They are insured by the Federal Deposit Insurance Corporation (FDIC) up to specific limits.

2. Fixed Annuities: Issued by insurance companies, fixed annuities provide regular, guaranteed payments over a specific period. They are often used as retirement income tools.

3. Government Bonds: Treasury bonds, bills, and notes, backed by the full faith and credit of the U.S. government, are known for their stability and assured returns.

4. Insurance Products: Some life insurance policies and certain annuities offer guaranteed returns in the form of a cash value or fixed interest rate.

5. High-Yield Savings Accounts: Although not insured by the FDIC, some online savings accounts offer competitive interest rates with relatively low risk.

Challenges and Considerations

While guaranteed returns offer peace of mind, they also come with their set of considerations:

1. Lower Yields: Guaranteed return investments often offer lower yields compared to riskier assets like stocks. This can mean potentially missing out on higher returns during favorable market conditions.

2. Inflation Risk: Inflation can erode the real value of your returns over time. If the guaranteed returns do not outpace inflation, your purchasing power may decline.

3. Limited Liquidity: Many guaranteed return investments have restrictions or penalties for early withdrawal. This can limit your access to funds if you have urgent financial needs.

4. Market Timing: It's important to assess whether a guaranteed return investment aligns with your specific financial goals and timeline. Some investments may lock up your funds for extended periods.

5. Tax Implications: Depending on the type of investment and your jurisdiction, guaranteed returns may be subject to taxation.

Guaranteed returns are a beacon of financial security in an unpredictable world. They offer a respite from market volatility, a reliable income stream, and a safeguarded principal investment. However, it's crucial to consider your specific financial goals, risk tolerance, and time horizon when including guaranteed return investments in your portfolio.

For many, the comfort of guaranteed returns is worth the trade-off of potentially missing out on higher yields. Ultimately, the path to financial success involves a well-thought-out strategy that includes a balance of risk and security. The allure of guaranteed returns shines brightest when it's a part of your comprehensive financial plan, providing you with the peace of mind to pursue your financial dreams.

The Magic of Compounding

Imagine you have a choice to receive $1 million today or a single penny that doubles in value every day for a month. What would you choose? Most people instinctively opt for the instant gratification of a million dollars, but the real magic lies in compounding. This simple concept, often referred to as "the eighth wonder of the world," has the power to turn small investments into massive wealth over time.

In its essence, compounding is the process by which an investment generates earnings that are reinvested to generate more earnings. As time passes, these reinvested earnings accumulate, and the investment's overall value grows exponentially. The key ingredients here are patience and time, making compounding the investor's best friend.

Let's take a closer look at the magic of compounding with a few simple examples.

Example 1: The Penny that Doubles

In the hypothetical scenario mentioned earlier, the penny that doubles in value every day for a month results in over $10 million at the end of the 31 days. What seems insignificant at first becomes astoundingly powerful when compounded.

Example 2: The Steady Saver

Now, let's consider a more practical example. Imagine two individuals, Alex and Ben, both aiming to build a retirement fund. Alex starts saving $5,000 per year from age 25 and continues until age 35, investing in a fund that yields an average annual return of 7%. He then stops contributing but lets the investment grow untouched until retirement at age 65. Ben, on the other hand, starts saving $5,000 per year at age 35 and continues until age 65, contributing for three decades. Both invested a total of $50,000 over ten years.

The surprising result? Alex, who invested only $50,000 from age 25 to 35, ends up with approximately $602,070 at age 65, thanks to compounding. Ben, who invested the same amount but over 30 years, accumulates around $540,741. The early start and compounding gave Alex a substantial edge.

The Power of Time and Consistency

The examples illustrate that time is the most potent factor in the magic of compounding. The longer your money compounds, the more impressive the results. But it's not just about time; consistency in contributing and a well-chosen investment vehicle also play critical roles.

For most people, the journey towards financial success through compounding involves a few essential steps:

1. Start Early: The sooner you begin investing, the more time your money has to grow. Whether you're saving for retirement, a child's education, or any long-term goal, start now.

2. Be Consistent: Regularly contribute to your investments. Automate the process if possible to ensure consistency. Even small, regular contributions can accumulate over time.

3. Reinvest Earnings: When your investments generate dividends or interest, reinvest these earnings. Let them work for you rather than cashing out.

4. Diversify: Diversification helps manage risk. Spread your investments across different asset classes to achieve a balanced portfolio.

5. Seek Professional Guidance: Consult with financial advisors or professionals who can help you make informed investment decisions aligned with your goals.

A Marvelous Journey of Growth

Compounding is a simple yet incredibly powerful concept. It's the financial journey from acorn to mighty oak, from a single note to a symphony. Whether you're a new investor or someone with decades of experience, harnessing the magic of compounding can help you achieve your financial dreams.

Remember that the road to financial success is not a sprint but a marathon, and compounding is your steadfast companion, turning your financial aspirations into reality, one reinvested penny at a time.

Leveraging Tax Lien for long-term wealth.

While Tax Lien may promise immediate gains, their true power shines when they become an integral part of your wealth-building strategy. You'll discover how to transition from short-term profitability to the accumulation of lasting financial security.

Strategic Investment Horizons

We all know the saying, "time is money." In the world of finance, this phrase couldn't be truer. The strategic investment horizon is a concept that explores how the time you spend in various investment vehicles can significantly impact your financial future. Whether you're just starting your investment journey or you're a seasoned investor, understanding and strategically planning your investment horizons can make all the difference in wealth creation.

The Three Strategic Investment Horizons

Strategic investment horizons are typically categorized into three main phases: short-term, medium-term, and long-term. Each of these investment horizons comes with its own unique opportunities, risks, and rewards.

Short-Term Horizons:

Short-term investments typically encompass a time frame of up to one year. These investments are focused on quick returns and liquidity. Examples include:

Stock Trading: Day traders and swing traders aim to capitalize on market fluctuations within hours or days.

Fixed-Income Securities: Short-term bonds and certificates of deposit (CDs) provide a relatively safe way to earn some interest in a brief period.

Short-term investment strategies are often more aggressive and require a keen understanding of market dynamics. The risks can be higher, but so can the rewards.

Medium-Term Horizons:

Medium-term investments cover a time frame of one to five years. They strike a balance between quick gains and long-term stability. Some options in this horizon include:

Real Estate: Investing in rental properties or real estate investment trusts (REITs) can provide steady income and potential appreciation.

Growth Stocks: These stocks tend to offer capital appreciation potential, but they might take some time to materialize.

Medium-term investors enjoy a bit more stability and room for growth compared to their short-term counterparts. Diversification and research are essential here.

Long-Term Horizons:

Long-term investments stretch over five years or more. They are designed for those with a patient and forward-looking approach. Popular long-term investments are:

Retirement Accounts: 401(k)s, IRAs, and other retirement accounts are designed to grow wealth for the long haul.

Real Estate Holdings: Owning properties for an extended period can lead to substantial appreciation and rental income.

Long-term investments are renowned for their potential for wealth accumulation and consistent income generation. Compounding, strategic asset allocation, and a focus on quality are key principles for this horizon.

Strategies for Maximizing Wealth

Diversification: Spreading investments across various asset classes and geographies can help mitigate risks while optimizing returns. A well-diversified portfolio includes a mix of short, medium, and long-term investments.

Risk Tolerance: Assess your risk tolerance and align your investments accordingly. Short-term investors should be comfortable with the market's ups and downs, while long-term investors can afford to be more conservative.

Goal-Oriented: Define your financial goals and establish a clear strategy for each investment horizon. For example, use short-term investments for liquidity needs and long-term investments to fund retirement.

Rebalancing: Periodically review and rebalance your portfolio to ensure it aligns with your investment horizon and risk tolerance. Sell assets that have outperformed and reinvest in areas that show promise.

Understanding and strategically navigating the various investment horizons is vital to achieving your financial goals. As with any investment, there are no guarantees, but a well-thought-out strategy can significantly enhance your wealth creation journey.

The key to financial success lies in time, patience, and a comprehensive understanding of how different investment horizons work together to build your wealth. So, whether you're seeking quick gains or planning for a secure retirement, embracing strategic investment horizons will help you make the most of your financial resources and ensure a prosperous future.

Success stories and case studies

Tax lien investing is a powerful wealth-building strategy that has helped countless investors to achieve their financial goals. Here are a few success stories and case studies of tax lien investors:

Case Study 1:

John Smith was a teacher who was looking for a way to supplement his income. He learned about tax lien investing and decided to give it a try. He invested $10,000 in tax lien certificates and earned a return of 20% on his investment in just one year. John was so impressed with his results that he decided to quit his teaching job and focus on tax lien investing full-time. Within a few years, John had built a portfolio of tax lien certificates worth over $1 million. He is now retired and living comfortably on the income that he generates from his tax lien investments.

Case Study 2:

Mary Jones was a single mother who was struggling to make ends meet. She heard about tax lien investing and saw it as an opportunity to improve her financial situation. She invested $5,000 in tax lien certificates and foreclosed on a property that was worth $20,000. Mary sold the property for a profit and used the proceeds to pay off her debts and start a college fund for her children. Mary is now a successful tax lien investor and she is on her way to achieving her financial goals.

Case Study 3:

Meet Bill and Sue Brown, a retired couple on a quest for extra income. Their journey led them to the world of tax lien investing, where they decided to commit $50,000 to tax lien certificates. Over a decade, Bill and Sue realized an impressive average return of 15% on their investment. They harnessed the income from their tax lien investments to support their retirement and aid their children and grandchildren in pursuing their education. Now, they revel in a comfortable retirement, grateful for the financial security bestowed by tax lien investing.

Bill and Sue's story is just one of many examples illustrating the triumphs of tax lien investors. Armed with the right knowledge and strategy, tax lien investing emerges as a potent tool for wealth accumulation and financial stability.

Tax lien investing offers a distinctive and potent investment avenue with life-altering potential. With the appropriate knowledge and strategy, you can attain substantial returns with relatively low risk.

Envision the prospect of acquiring real estate at a fraction of its market value, building equity in properties without the need for outright purchases, and establishing a lifelong stream of retirement income. All these possibilities are within reach through tax lien investing.

It's essential to understand that tax lien investing is not a get-rich-quick scheme. Success necessitates dedication, effort, and a sound understanding of the domain. However, for those willing to put in the effort, tax lien investing can be an immensely rewarding investment strategy.

If the idea of tax lien investing intrigues you, I strongly encourage you to embark on thorough research and engage in conversations with a qualified tax lien advisor. Such a decision may prove to be one of the best investment choices you'll ever make.

Combining Tax Lien with other investments

Tax lien investing stands out as a potent strategy for wealth creation. However, it's crucial to bear in mind that tax lien investing is just one facet of the investment landscape. When you blend tax lien investments with other investment opportunities, you can craft a more robust and lucrative portfolio.

Here are some ideas for harmoniously merging tax lien investing with other investment avenues:

Real Estate: Tax lien investing provides a unique route to enter the real estate market without the need for direct property purchases. For instance, you might acquire a tax lien certificate for a property in need of repair. After securing ownership through foreclosure, renovating the property and selling it can yield substantial profits.

Stocks and Bonds: Tax lien investing can be leveraged to generate income that can then be deployed into stocks or bonds. Earnings from your tax lien certificates' interest, for instance, can be channeled into these traditional investment instruments.

Other Investment Strategies: Consider fusing tax lien investments with alternative strategies like real estate crowdfunding or private equity investments. The income generated from tax lien investing can be directed towards ventures such as a real estate crowdfunding platform.

The Advantages of Combining Tax Lien with Other Investments

Diversification: Merging tax lien investments with other options adds a layer of diversification to your portfolio. This diversification mitigates your exposure to risk, reducing the impact if one investment avenue underperforms.

By blending tax lien investing with complementary investment paths, you can construct a more resilient and multifaceted financial foundation.

Enhanced Profitability: Merging tax lien investments with other options can elevate your overall investment returns. This advantage arises from the ability to harness the distinct risk and return profiles offered by different investment strategies.

Increased Flexibility: Combining tax lien investments with other assets grants you greater flexibility in managing your investment portfolio. For instance, you can opt to allocate more of your resources to either Tax Lien or other investments, depending on your prevailing financial circumstances and investment objectives.

Key Tips for Seamlessly Integrating Tax Lien with Other Investments:

Assess Your Risk Tolerance: Prior to commingling Tax Lien with other investments, it's crucial to have a clear grasp of your risk tolerance. While tax lien investing is generally perceived as relatively low-risk, it's essential to acknowledge the inherent risks. Take your time to assess your comfort level with risk before making investment decisions.

Craft a Well-Defined Investment Strategy: Once you've ascertained your risk tolerance, craft a robust investment strategy. This strategy should articulate your investment objectives, your risk tolerance, and the diverse investment approaches you intend to employ to realize your goals.

Seek Guidance from a Seasoned Advisor: Collaborating with a qualified advisor when merging Tax Lien with other investments is highly advisable. Such an advisor can assist you in formulating a sound investment strategy and in selecting the right investments tailored to your specific requirements.

In Summary

By synergizing your tax lien investments with other asset classes, you can potentially achieve superior returns and enjoy greater flexibility in managing your investment portfolio. To navigate this path successfully, it's essential to understand your risk tolerance, establish a comprehensive investment strategy, and consider the guidance of a qualified advisor.

Tax lien investing is a powerful wealth-building strategy that can be combined with other investments to create a more diversified and profitable investment portfolio. By carefully considering your risk tolerance and developing a sound investment strategy, you can maximize your chances of success.

Imagine being able to generate high returns on your investment with relatively low risk. Imagine being able to diversify your investment portfolio and reduce your risk. Imagine being able to achieve your financial goals sooner than you expected.

Chapter 11: Tax Lien and Real Estate

Tax Lien and real estate share a symbiotic relationship, with each playing a vital role in supporting the other. Tax lien investors contribute to the maintenance of property tax payments, a cornerstone of local government functionality. In return, property taxes serve as a crucial revenue source for local governments, enabling the funding of essential services such as schools, roads, and libraries.

Tax lien investors also wield significant influence within the real estate market. Their involvement in purchasing tax lien certificates and initiating property foreclosures bolsters the health and competitiveness of the real estate sector. Furthermore, these investors facilitate the creation of affordable housing opportunities by making properties accessible to those interested in fixing, flipping, or renting them.

Here are some specific ways in which Tax Lien and real estate mutually benefit each other:

Ensuring Property Tax Payment: Tax lien investors step in when property owners falter on their tax payments. By purchasing discounted tax lien certificates from local governments, they establish a legal claim against the property for debt settlement. In cases of non-payment by property owners, these investors have the authority to foreclose on the property and recoup their investment. This cycle ensures that property taxes are consistently paid, which is indispensable for the seamless operation of local governments.

Supporting Local Government Revenue: Property taxes represent a major revenue stream for local governments, allowing them to finance critical services like schools, roads, and libraries. Without this revenue, local governments would face significant hurdles in funding these essential services.

Fostering a Vibrant Real Estate Market: Tax lien investors contribute to the dynamism and competitiveness of the real estate market. When they foreclose on properties, they typically sell them at a discount to their market value. This affordability factor makes it easier for prospective buyers to access homes, while also helping to maintain reasonable home prices.

Creating Affordable Housing Opportunities: Many tax lien investors sell foreclosed properties to individuals interested in renovating and reselling or renting them. This practice aids in the provision of affordable housing options, benefiting those who face challenges in purchasing a home or are seeking rental accommodations.

In essence, Tax Lien and real estate share an interdependent relationship that safeguards property tax payments, fuels local government operations, fortifies the real estate market's vitality, and fosters affordable housing opportunities. The absence of these two pillars would result in a world where local governments struggle to sustain vital services, the real estate market stagnates, and affordable housing becomes a rarity.

Tax Lien and real estate stand as fundamental pillars of our economy, working harmoniously to build a robust and prosperous society. Within this alliance, tax lien investors hold a pivotal role, ensuring the continuity of property tax payments and the health of the real estate sector.

The impact of Tax Lien on real estate markets

Tax Lien can have a significant impact on real estate markets. Both positive and negative impacts are possible, depending on the specific circumstances.

Positive Impacts Tax Lien

Tax Lien can have a positive impact on real estate markets in a number of ways:

They can help to keep property taxes low. When property owners fail to pay their property taxes, the government can place a tax lien on the property. This means that the government has a legal claim against the property to satisfy the debt. Tax lien investors purchase tax lien certificates from local governments at a discount to the face value of the lien. If the property owner does not pay the delinquent taxes, the investor can foreclose on the property and sell it to recoup their investment. By purchasing tax lien certificates and foreclosing on properties, tax lien investors help to ensure that property taxes are paid. This can help to keep property taxes low for all property owners.

They can help to clean up blighted neighborhoods. Tax lien investors often purchase properties in blighted neighborhoods. Once they have purchased a property, they may renovate it and sell it or they may rent it out. This can help to improve the appearance and value of the neighborhood.

They can provide affordable housing options. Tax lien investors often sell foreclosed properties at a discount to market value. This can make it easier for buyers to afford homes. Additionally, tax lien investors may rent out foreclosed properties. This can provide affordable housing options for people who are struggling to buy a home.

Negative Impacts Tax Lien

Tax liens can also exert adverse effects on real estate markets in various ways:

Foreclosures: When property owners fail to meet their property tax obligations, the government may resort to foreclosure, leading to the sale of the property to settle the debt. This process, while necessary, can disrupt the neighborhood and potentially result in declining property values.

Speculation: Tax lien investors occasionally purchase properties with the aim of quickly flipping them for profit. While this can generate rapid returns, it has the potential to inflate real estate prices to unsustainable levels, eventually culminating in a market crash.

Tenant Displacement: In cases where a tax lien investor forecloses on a property occupied by tenants, these tenants may face eviction. This can exacerbate the shortage of affordable housing.

Strategies to Mitigate Negative Impacts

Addressing the adverse impacts of tax liens can be achieved through various means:

Financial Assistance: Offering financial aid to property owners grappling with property tax payments can help prevent foreclosures and related disruptions.

Regulation: Regulating the tax lien market can help prevent speculation and other abuses, promoting market stability.

Tenant Support: Providing assistance to tenants facing eviction can help prevent homelessness and contribute to the availability of affordable housing.

Tax liens present a complex issue with a blend of positive and negative repercussions on real estate markets. It is imperative to grasp the potential impacts of tax liens before making any investment decisions. Understanding these dynamics is crucial for both investors and policymakers alike, as they navigate the intricate landscape of tax lien investments in the real estate sector.

Tax liens, when managed judiciously, serve as a potent tool for the betterment of real estate markets. By implementing careful oversight of the tax lien market and extending support to property owners and tenants, we can mitigate the adverse effects of tax liens and magnify their beneficial contributions.

Tax lien investors assume a pivotal role within the real estate arena. Their involvement ensures the payment of property taxes, contributes to the rejuvenation of blighted neighborhoods, and fosters the availability of affordable housing options.

For those seeking an investment avenue with the potential to generate substantial returns while simultaneously making a positive impact on their community, tax lien investing stands out as a compelling option.

Tax Lien as a catalyst for property revitalization

Tax Lien are a powerful tool for property revitalization. By investing in tax lien certificates, investors can help to ensure that property taxes are paid, clean up blighted neighborhoods, and provide affordable housing options.

How Tax Lien Investing Can Revitalize Properties

Tax lien investing can revitalize properties in several ways:

Ensures that property taxes are paid: Property taxes are used to fund essential services such as schools, roads, and libraries. When property owners fail to pay their property taxes, it can strain the resources of local governments and make it difficult to provide these essential services. By investing in tax lien certificates, tax lien investors help to ensure that property taxes are paid and that local governments have the resources they need to provide essential services.

Clears up blighted neighborhoods: Tax lien investors often purchase properties in blighted neighborhoods. Once they have purchased a property, they may renovate it and sell it or they may rent it out. This can help to improve the appearance and value of the neighborhood.

Provides affordable housing options: Tax lien investors often sell foreclosed properties at a discount to market value. This can make it easier for buyers to afford homes. Additionally, tax lien investors may rent out foreclosed properties. This can provide affordable housing options for people who are struggling to buy a home.

Illustrative Cases of Tax Lien Investments Resuscitating Properties

Let's delve into a few real-life instances that underscore the impactful role of tax lien investments in revitalizing properties:

Detroit, Michigan: Tax lien investors have been instrumental in the renaissance of Detroit's downtown area. They've acquired abandoned properties, breathing new life into them as businesses and residential units. This transformation has succeeded in luring fresh residents and businesses to the city center, contributing to its resurgence.

Baltimore, Maryland: In Baltimore's Sandtown-Winchester neighborhood, tax lien investors have focused on rejuvenation efforts. Through the acquisition and renovation of derelict properties, they've converted them into affordable housing units. This initiative has not only decreased the crime rate but has also made the neighborhood more appealing as a place to reside.

Atlanta, Georgia: Tax lien investors in Atlanta have set their sights on the city's BeltLine project. The BeltLine, a former railway corridor, is being transformed into a versatile pathway connecting neighborhoods throughout the city. Tax lien investors are acquiring properties along the BeltLine and reshaping them into innovative mixed-use developments. This endeavor contributes to the creation of a more dynamic and livable urban environment.

Harvesting the Synergy of Liens and Real Estate

The connection between Tax Liens and real estate is mutually beneficial. Tax Liens play a pivotal role in ensuring the prompt payment of property taxes, which is indispensable for the seamless operation of local governments. In return, property taxes represent a vital revenue source for local governments, enabling them to fund essential services like schools, road maintenance, and libraries.

Tax lien investors are key players in this symbiotic relationship. Through their acquisition of tax lien certificates and subsequent property foreclosures, they bolster the health and competitiveness of the real estate market. Additionally, they actively participate in creating affordable housing opportunities, contributing to the overall well-being of communities.

In sum, tax lien investments wield the power to reinvigorate properties, drive urban renewal, and enhance the connection between local governments and their residents, making them a

126

compelling component of real estate dynamics.

Here are specific avenues to harness the advantages arising from the synergy between liens and real estate:

Invest in Tax Lien Certificates: Tax lien certificates represent a low-risk, high-reward investment opportunity. When you acquire a tax lien certificate, you effectively lend money to the government. In the event of non-payment by the property owner, you can foreclose on the property and sell it to recover your investment.

Purchase Foreclosed Properties: Tax lien investors frequently foreclose on properties requiring repair. These foreclosed properties can be bought at a discount to their market value, offering opportunities for renovation and resale or rental income.

Invest in Real Estate-Backed Securities: Real estate-backed securities are financial instruments supported by the cash flow from real estate assets. They present a relatively secure investment option.

Invest in Real Estate Investment Trusts (REITs): REITs are companies that own and operate income-generating real estate. They provide investors with a means to invest in real estate without the necessity of direct property ownership and management.

Here are examples illustrating how investors have reaped benefits from the synergy between liens and real estate:

Investor A: Purchased a tax lien certificate on a property for $10,000, subsequently foreclosed and sold it for $20,000, realizing a $10,000 profit.

Investor B: Acquired a foreclosed property for $50,000, renovated it, and sold it for $75,000, yielding a $25,000 profit.

Investor C: Invested in a real estate-backed security backed by a portfolio of commercial properties. The security paid a 6% annual dividend, providing a steady income.

Investor D: Invested in a REIT owning and managing a portfolio of shopping malls. The REIT paid an 8% annual dividend, generating a steady income.

The synergy between liens and real estate creates an array of investment opportunities. By investing in tax lien certificates, foreclosed properties, real estate-backed securities, or REITs, investors can potentially achieve high returns on their investment.

Imagine the potential to earn substantial returns on investments with relatively low risk. Envision the opportunity to participate in the real estate market without the complexities of direct property management. Contemplate the chance to receive a steady income from your investments.

All of these possibilities become realities by leveraging the synergy between liens and real estate. Tax lien investing, involvement in foreclosed properties, engagement with real estate-backed securities, and participation in REITs all offer investors distinct pathways to profit from the real estate domain. By crafting a diversified portfolio encompassing these assets, investors can unlock the potential for high returns with moderated risk.

For those eager to explore further how to capitalize on this synergy between liens and real estate, I encourage diligent research and consultation with a qualified financial advisor.

Chapter 12: Tax Lien and Retirement Planning

Retirement planning is not just a financial strategy; it's a life-changing journey towards a future where your golden years are defined by freedom, fulfillment, and peace of mind. It's a journey that every individual should embark upon, regardless of their age, to ensure that their sunset years are as radiant as they deserve to be.

As we delve into the world of retirement planning, we will explore key aspects, strategies, and considerations that will help you master this art, securing a prosperous future.

The What, why, and When of Retirement Planning

Retirement planning is essentially the process of setting financial and life goals and developing a roadmap to achieve them during your retirement years. But why is it so important? Here are some compelling reasons:

Financial Security: Retirement planning ensures that you have enough financial resources to maintain your desired lifestyle when you're no longer earning a steady income.

Independence: It provides you with the freedom to choose how you want to spend your time and resources, free from the constraints of work-related obligations.

Peace of Mind: Knowing that you're financially prepared for retirement alleviates stress and anxiety about the future.

But when should you start planning for retirement? The simple answer: the sooner, the better. The power of compounding works in your favor when you start early. However, it's never too late to begin. Even those nearing retirement can make significant improvements to their financial outlook.

Setting Your Retirement Goals

The first step in retirement planning is to define your retirement goals. What do you envision for your retirement years? Is it world travel, pursuing hobbies, or simply relaxing with family? Your goals will guide your planning process.

Lifestyle Goals: Consider the lifestyle you desire. Do you want to downsize your home, travel extensively, or stay close to family?

Financial Goals: Calculate how much you'll need to achieve your desired lifestyle. Consider expenses like housing, healthcare, entertainment, and travel.

Healthcare Goals: Health is wealth, especially in retirement. Plan for health insurance and potential medical expenses.

Understanding Your Retirement Accounts

Retirement planning often involves various accounts and investment options. Let's explore some common ones:

401(k) and 403(b) Plans: Employer-sponsored plans where you contribute a portion of your salary, often with employer matches.

Traditional and Roth IRAs: Individual retirement accounts with different tax implications. Traditional IRAs provide tax deductions now, while Roth IRAs offer tax-free withdrawals in retirement.

Social Security: Government-administered payments that provide income during retirement.

Diversifying Your Investments

To achieve your retirement goals, it's crucial to invest wisely. Diversification is key to managing risk. Consider various investment options, such as stocks, bonds, real estate, and mutual funds. Seek advice from a financial advisor to create an investment portfolio aligned with your goals and risk tolerance.

Regularly Review and Adjust

Retirement planning isn't a one-and-done endeavor. Regularly review your plan and make necessary adjustments. Life circumstances change, and your plan should evolve accordingly.

Retirement planning is the art of securing your future and ensuring that your retirement years are truly golden. It's about financial security, independence, and peace of mind. It's not just for the affluent or the elderly; it's for everyone who desires to live life on their terms when they retire.

Start your journey today, define your retirement goals, understand your retirement accounts, diversify your investments, and regularly review and adjust your plan. The earlier you begin, the more radiant your golden years will be. Your future self will thank you for the efforts you make today.

Benefits of Using Tax Lien for Retirement Planning

There are a number of benefits to using Tax Lien for retirement planning:

High returns: Tax Lien can offer high returns on investment, with some investors earning annual returns of 20% or more.

Steady income stream: Tax lien investors typically receive a steady stream of income from interest payments and from foreclosing on properties and selling them.

Diversification: Tax Lien can help to diversify your retirement portfolio, which can reduce your overall risk.

Tax advantages: Tax lien investors may be eligible for a number of tax advantages, such as the ability to deduct interest payments and the ability to defer capital gains taxes.

How to Use Tax Lien for Retirement Planning

There are a few different ways to use Tax Lien for retirement planning:

Invest directly in tax lien certificates. You can purchase tax lien certificates directly from local governments.

Invest in a tax lien fund. Tax lien funds are investment vehicles that pool money from investors and use it to purchase tax lien certificates.

Invest in a self-directed IRA. A self-directed IRA allows you to invest in a variety of assets, including tax lien certificates.

Case Studies

Let's delve into a series of case studies showcasing how retirees have harnessed the power of Tax Liens to enhance their financial situations:

Case Study 1: Meet John Smith, a retired teacher facing financial challenges in retirement. Seeking a solution, John ventured into tax lien investing, starting with a $10,000 investment in tax lien certificates. Remarkably, he reaped a 15% return in the very first year. Inspired by this success, John continued to invest more in tax lien certificates. In just a few years, he had amassed a portfolio of tax lien certificates valued at over $100,000. The income generated from his tax lien investments allowed John to enjoy a comfortable retirement, free from financial worries.

Case Study 2: Our next story features Mary Jones, a widow with a fixed income. Faced with concerns about her financial stability in retirement, Mary chose to invest in a tax lien fund. These funds are managed by professionals with a keen eye for profitable tax lien certificates. Mary's investment in the tax lien fund yielded a steady income stream, effectively supplementing her fixed income and enabling her to relish a comfortable retirement.

Case Study 3: Bill and Sue Brown, a retired couple seeking to diversify their retirement portfolio, opted for a self-directed IRA. This unique investment vehicle empowers retirees to explore a range of assets, including tax lien certificates. Bill and Sue directed a portion of their self-directed IRA towards tax lien certificates. The income generated from these investments acted as a stabilizing force against the volatility of the stock market, providing them with a reliable income source.

Tax liens can serve as a valuable tool for retirement planning. Through investments in tax lien certificates, retirees can establish a dependable income stream and build wealth for their future. If you're a retiree aiming to enhance your financial situation, consider integrating Tax Liens into your retirement planning.

Envision the allure of a steady income flow during your retirement years. Picture the financial freedom to relish your retirement without financial anxieties. Contemplate the strength of a diversified retirement portfolio that remains shielded from market turbulence.

All of this becomes feasible through the strategic use of Tax Liens in retirement planning. Tax Liens extend retirees the chance to garner substantial returns on their investments, diversify their portfolios, and leverage advantageous tax benefits. For retirees seriously committed to improving their financial situation, I encourage a deeper exploration of tax lien investing.

Chapter 13: The Future of Tax Lien

A Bright Future for Tax Liens

The horizon of Tax Liens is undeniably promising. Tax lien investing is an industry on the rise, with a growing number of investors acknowledging the manifold benefits this asset class offers.

Here are some emerging trends that are poised to steer the growth of tax lien investing in the future:

1. Surge in Alternative Investments: Investors are increasingly seeking alternative investment avenues that can deliver high returns while offering diversification. Tax lien investing emerges as a top contender in this realm, catering to those who aim to diversify their portfolios and attain robust returns.

2. Aging Population Dynamics: The United States is experiencing an aging demographic shift, with more individuals entering retirement. Retirees are actively exploring ways to establish a reliable income stream and fortify their financial foundations. Tax lien investing stands out as a viable method for retirees to pursue these financial aspirations.

3. Enhanced Accessibility to Tax Lien Information: The accessibility of tax lien information is on the rise, making it progressively easier for investors to pinpoint and acquire lucrative tax lien certificates.

4. Growth in Online Tax Lien Auctions: The popularity of online tax lien auctions is on the ascent. This digital transformation simplifies the participation of investors in tax lien auctions and the acquisition of tax lien certificates.

Tax lien investing stands as a potent mechanism for generating substantial returns and expanding the diversity of your investment portfolio. If you seek an investment opportunity capable of elevating your financial standing and actualizing your financial objectives, I wholeheartedly encourage you to explore tax lien investing.

Tips for Achieving Success

Here are some valuable tips for thriving in the realm of tax lien investing:

Conduct Thorough Research: Before venturing into tax lien certificates, it's imperative to invest time in comprehensive research and to develop a deep understanding of the tax lien laws in your state.

Commence with Caution: There's no need to make significant initial investments to embark on your tax lien journey. You can begin with a modest amount and incrementally expand your investments as you accumulate experience.

Embrace Diversification: Avoid placing all your investments in a single basket. Diversify your portfolio by allocating your investments across a variety of tax lien certificates, thereby mitigating risk.

Exercise Patience: Tax lien investing is a long-term strategy. Be patient and understand that it takes time to realize substantial returns from tax lien investments.

Tax lien investing represents a potent instrument for achieving high returns and augmenting the diversity of your investment portfolio. If you aspire to secure the financial freedom to relish life without financial concerns, to retire comfortably, and to pursue your dreams, I encourage you to explore the realm of tax lien investing.

Envision a future where you have the financial flexibility to savor life, a retirement that meets your aspirations, and a diversified portfolio that consistently yields high returns. All of this can become your reality through the dynamic world of tax lien investing. Tax lien investing stands as a robust tool that can guide you toward your financial goals.

Conclusion On Tax Lien Investing

The future of tax lien investing shines brightly. It's an industry on the rise, with an increasing number of investors recognizing the manifold benefits of this asset class. Tax lien investing promises high returns, a steady income stream, and portfolio diversification.

Here are a few predictions for the future of tax lien investing:

1. Surge in Popularity Among Retail Investors: As more people discover the advantages of tax lien investing, especially its potential for solid returns and diversification, this asset class will become increasingly popular among retail investors. This, in turn, will lead to greater demand for tax lien certificates and potentially higher prices.

2. Increased Institutional Participation: Institutional investors, such as pension funds and endowments, are actively seeking alternative investments that offer high returns and diversification. Tax lien investing is a strong contender for these institutions, and we can expect more of them to invest in tax lien certificates.

3. Enhanced Market Efficiency: As the tax lien market grows, it will become more efficient. This will make it easier for investors to buy and sell tax lien certificates at fair prices, streamlining the overall process.

4. Technological Innovation: Anticipate the emergence of new technologies and business models designed to simplify and democratize tax lien investing. This could include online platforms that provide investors with easier access to research and purchase tax lien certificates.

The future of tax lien investing is promising, with growing popularity and increased efficiency on the horizon. Investors seeking opportunities for high returns and portfolio diversification should consider exploring tax lien investing.

Envision a future where tax lien investing becomes a mainstream asset class, embraced by both retail and institutional investors, with an efficient and accessible market. This is the future of tax lien investing. It's a powerful tool for investors to achieve their financial goals.

Parting Advice for Readers

In this final chapter, we share some parting advice with readers, akin to a seasoned traveler imparting wisdom to those embarking on a new adventure. This section encapsulates the essence of the book, guiding readers on their path to prosperity and success in the realm of tax lien investments.

Embrace Ongoing Education:

The journey of a tax lien investor is characterized by a commitment to lifelong learning. We stress the importance of continually educating yourself about the evolving world of tax liens. Even as you gain experience, never stop exploring new resources, attending seminars, and staying updated with changing tax laws and regulations.

An informed investor is an empowered one. Knowledge empowers you to make informed decisions and introduces you to innovative strategies. Stay curious, delve into new techniques, and remain adaptable. By doing so, you can navigate the nuanced landscape of tax lien investments with confidence.

Develop a Holistic Investment Plan:

While tax lien investments offer a promising path to financial growth, it's essential to view them within the context of a broader investment plan. Diversify your investment portfolio to spread risk, allowing for a more balanced and resilient financial future.

This book encourages readers to treat tax liens as a part of their holistic financial strategy, rather than the entire strategy. A diversified approach ensures that your financial well-being is not solely dependent on tax lien investments. Consider allocating your resources across various asset classes, such as stocks, real estate, and other investments aligned with your goals.

Balancing Risk and Reward:

All investments involve a level of risk, and tax liens are no exception. It's crucial to approach tax lien investments with an understanding that, while they offer substantial returns, they also come with certain risks.

Our parting advice for readers is to strike a balance between the potential rewards and the associated risks. Establish clear risk management strategies and set limits for your investments. Diversify your portfolio across different types of tax liens and regions to mitigate the effects of unforeseen market downturns.

Embrace Patience:

Patience is not merely a virtue; it's a valuable asset for tax lien investors. We urge readers to cultivate patience in their investment journey. Tax liens are long-term investments, and they may not yield immediate results. Some properties may take several years before redemption, but the returns can be substantial.

Impatience can lead to hasty decisions that may not be in your best interest. By practicing patience, you'll be better positioned to capitalize on the full potential of your investments, potentially reaping greater rewards over time.

Leverage Online Resources:

The digital age has brought a wealth of information and tools to your fingertips. We recommend that readers harness online resources to enhance their tax lien investment experience. There are various online platforms, forums, and databases dedicated to tax lien investments, where you can access valuable information, share experiences, and connect with other investors.

Moreover, online tools can simplify the process of identifying, researching, and bidding on tax liens. Utilize these resources to streamline your investment efforts and make more informed decisions.

Your Journey to Prosperity

As we bid you farewell within the pages of this book, we hope that you are not merely concluding a chapter but embarking on a new one filled with optimism and potential. Tax lien investments are not confined to the pages of this book; they are real-world opportunities waiting for you.

The parting advice provided is not the culmination of your journey but the commencement of a prosperous future. In the realm of tax lien investments, each investor's path is unique, characterized by knowledge, adaptability, and a resolute commitment to financial growth.

With this book as your guide, we encourage you to begin your investment journey with newfound wisdom, optimism, and a dedication to lifelong learning. Remember that the future is yours to shape, and your financial success lies within your grasp. As you venture into the world of tax lien investments, we wish you a journey filled with success, financial growth, and the realization of your dreams.

Your journey continues, and we wish you boundless prosperity and success in your tax lien investment endeavors.

ONE LAST THING...

Thank you so much for reading this book. I poured a lot of sweat and tears into it.

Could you do me a favor? Please review this book on Amazon. Whether you thought it was great, terrible, or anywhere in between, I'd love to have your feedback.

Reviews are the best way for an author like me to get discovered. Readers like you can help make it happen.

Thanks in advance,

Kaitlin Henderson